Lecture Notes in Computer Science 15525

Founding Editors

Gerhard Goos

Juris Hartmanis

The series Lecture Notes in Computer Science (LNCS), including its subseries Lecture Notes in Artificial Intelligence (LNAI) and Lecture Notes in Bioinformatics (LNBI), has established itself as a medium for the publication of new developments in computer science and information technology research, teaching, and education.

LNCS enjoys close cooperation with the computer science R & D community, the series counts many renowned academics among its volume editors and paper authors, and collaborates with prestigious societies. Its mission is to serve this international community by providing an invaluable service, mainly focused on the publication of conference and workshop proceedings and postproceedings. LNCS commenced publication in 1973.

Jonathan Protzenko · Azalea Raad
Editors

Verified Software

Theories, Tools and Experiments

16th International Conference, VSTTE 2024
Prague, Czech Republic, October 14–15, 2024
Revised Selected Papers

 Springer

Editors
Jonathan Protzenko ⓘ
Microsoft Azure Research
Redmond, WA, USA

Azalea Raad ⓘ
Imperial College London
South Kensington, UK

ISSN 0302-9743   ISSN 1611-3349 (electronic)
Lecture Notes in Computer Science
ISBN 978-3-031-86694-4   ISBN 978-3-031-86695-1 (eBook)
https://doi.org/10.1007/978-3-031-86695-1

This Springer imprint is published by the registered company Springer Nature Switzerland AG
The registered company address is: Gewerbestrasse 11, 6330 Cham, Switzerland

If disposing of this product, please recycle the paper.

Preface

This volume contains the papers presented at VSTTE 2024, the International Conference on Verified Software: Theories, Tools and Experiments, held on October 14–15, 2024 in Prague, Czech Republic. It was co-located with Formal Methods in Computer-Aided Design 2024.

The program included 6 papers chosen out of 6 submissions using double-blind reviews. Each submission was reviewed by 4 program committee members, on average. The program also included three invited talks and one invited tutorial. Cristian Cadar (Imperial College London) gave an invited talk titled "Dynamic Symbolic Execution: Between Testing and Verification". Karthikeyan Bhargavan (Cryspen and Inria) gave an invited talk titled "High-Assurance Post-quantum Cryptography". Igor Konnov gave an invited talk titled "Pragmatic Bounded Model Checking for TLA+ with Apalache". The proceedings additionally include an invited paper by Karthikeyan Bhargavan et al., which was individually reviewed by the PC chairs prior to inclusion. The conference was followed by an invited tutorial, given by Sebastian Ullrich and Joachim Breitner (Lean FRO), titled "The Lean Programming Language and Theorem Prover".

The goal of the VSTTE conference series is to advance the state of the art in the science and technology of software verification, through the interaction of theory development, tool evolution, and experimental validation.

The Verified Software Initiative (VSI), spearheaded by Tony Hoare and Jayadev Misra, is a research program for making large-scale verified software a practical reality. The International Conference on Verified Software: Theories, Tools, and Experiments (VSTTE) is the main forum for advancing the initiative. VSTTE brings together experts spanning the spectrum of software verification in order to foster international collaboration on the critical research challenges. The theoretical work includes semantic foundations and logics for specification and verification, and verification algorithms and methodologies. The tools cover specification and annotation languages, program analyzers, model checkers, interactive verifiers and proof checkers, automated theorem provers and SAT/SMT solvers, and integrated verification environments. The experimental work drives the research agenda for theory and tools by taking on significant specification/verification exercises covering hardware, operating systems, compilers, computer security, parallel computing, and cyber-physical systems.

December 2024

Jonathan Protzenko
Azalea Raad

Organization

Program Committee Chairs

Jonathan Protzenko	Microsoft Azure Research, USA
Azalea Raad	Imperial College, London

Steering Committee

Supratik Chakraborty	IIT Bombay, India
Natarajan Shankar	SRI International, USA

Program Committee

Andreas Loow	Imperial College London, UK
Arie Gurfinkel	University of Waterloo, Canada
Burcu Kulahcioglu Ozkan	TU Delft, Netherlands
Claire Dross	AdaCore, France
Emanuele D'Osualdo	University of Konstanz, Germany
Gregory Malecha	BlueRock Security, USA
Guillaume Ambal	Imperial College London, UK
Guy Amir	The Hebrew University of Jerusalem, Israel
John Wickerson	Imperial College London, UK
Joonwon Choi	Apple, USA
Juneyoung Lee	Amazon Web Services, USA
Karine Even Mendoza	King's College London, UK
Kartik Nagar	IIT Madras, India
Kenneth L. McMillan	University of Texas at Austin, USA
Kumar Madhukar	IIT Delhi, India
Léo Stefanesco	MPI-SWS, Germany
Marc Pouzet	ENS and Inria, France
Martin Bodin	Inria, France
Michael Sammler	MPI-SWS, Germany
Michalis Kokologiannakis	MPI-SWS, Germany
Paulo de Vilhena	Imperial College London, UK
Roland Meyer	TU Braunschweig, Germany
Rupak Majumdar	MPI-SWS, Germany

Soham Chakraborty   TU Delft, Netherlands
Umang Mathur   NUS, Singapore
Yu-Fang Chen   Academia Sinica, Taiwan

Contents

MoXIchecker:
An Extensible Model Checker for MoXI

Salih Ates[iD], Dirk Beyer[iD], Po-Chun Chien[iD], and Nian-Ze Lee[iD]

LMU Munich, Munich, Germany

Abstract. MoXI is a new intermediate verification language introduced in 2024 to promote the standardization and open-source implementations for symbolic model checking by extending the SMT-LIB 2 language with constructs to define state-transition systems. The tool suite of MoXI provides a translator from MoXI to Btor2, which is a lower-level intermediate language for hardware verification, and a translation-based model checker, which invokes mature hardware model checkers for Btor2 to analyze the translated verification tasks. The extensibility of such a translation-based model checker is restricted because more complex theories, such as integer or real arithmetics, cannot be precisely expressed with bit-vectors of fixed lengths in Btor2. We present MoXIchecker, the first model checker that solves MoXI verification tasks directly. Instead of translating MoXI to lower-level languages, MoXIchecker uses the solver-agnostic library PySMT for SMT solvers as backend for its verification algorithms. MoXIchecker is *extensible* because it accommodates verification tasks involving more complex theories, not limited by lower-level languages, facilitates the implementation of new algorithms, and is solver-agnostic by using the API of PySMT. In our evaluation, MoXIchecker uniquely solved tasks that use integer or real arithmetics, and achieved a comparable performance against the translation-based model checker from the MoXI tool suite.

Keywords: Formal verification · Symbolic model checking · Intermediate language · MoXI · Btor2 · SMT · SAT · PySMT · Exchange formats

1 Introduction

Symbolic model checking [1, 2] embraces a wide range of automatic techniques to formally verify a model against a specification by encoding and searching the state space symbolically. It has been applied to hardware, software, and cyber-physical systems to ensure their safety and correct functionality. However, symbolic model checking has not been adopted as widely as other "push-button" techniques for quality assurance, such as testing, especially in industry. A major challenge is the lack of standardized exchange formats and open-source implementations [3, 4]. Even though model checkers from the same research community work on the same type of computational models, they often use different input formats, which hinders the propagation of techniques. Moreover, some model checkers are closed-source and make the comparison of verification algorithms complicated, because

© The Author(s) 2025
J. Protzenko and A. Raad (Eds.): VSTTE 2024, LNCS 15525, pp. 1–14, 2025.
https://doi.org/10.1007/978-3-031-86695-1_1

techniques may need to be re-implemented in a different framework to achieve fair comparison (this makes expensive transferability studies necessary [5, 6]).

Recently, a new intermediate verification language MoXI [3], the *model exchange interlingua*, has been proposed to address the aforementioned challenge. MoXI aims to be (1) as expressive as necessary to accommodate real-world applications described in user-facing, higher-level modeling languages and (2) as simple as possible to facilitate its translation to tool-oriented, lower-level intermediate languages, for which efficient and effective model checkers are available. It augments the SMT-LIB 2 [7] format with constructs to define state-transition systems by using formulas in first-order logic to encode their initial and transition conditions. MoXI inherits the expressiveness of SMT-LIB 2 and offers abundant background theories to represent various computational models, ranging from hardware circuits and software programs to cyber-physical systems. The precise semantics of SMT-LIB 2 also enables the translation from MoXI to lower-level intermediate languages. Using SMT formulas to precisely describe state-transition systems has also been studied in the VMT [8] intermediate language.

Compared to other intermediate verification languages, such as the SMV [9] language for finite-state transition systems or the BOOGIE [10] language for software programs, using MoXI to represent model-checking problems frees backend verification engines from encoding the semantics of frontend modeling languages into SMT formulas. This separation of frontend and backend will help decompose monolithic model checkers into several modular and reusable components, e.g., standalone translators from higher-level frontend languages to MoXI and efficient model-checking engines for MoXI verification tasks. A deeper discussion can be found in a recent survey on transformation for verification [11].

1.1   Existing Tool Suite for MoXI

The tool suite of MoXI [12] offers translators from SMV to MoXI and from MoXI to the word-level modeling language BTOR2 [13], the prevailing format for hardware model checking. The tool suite also implements a translation-based model checker, MoXI-MC-FLOW, by translating a MoXI task to an equisatisfiable BTOR2 task and invoking BTOR2 model checkers, such as AVR [14], BTORMC [13], and PONO [15], on the translated task. Translation-based verification approaches have been actively studied in the literature. For example, sequential circuits in VERILOG [16] can be translated to SMV models [17, 18] or C programs [19] for verification. BTOR2 circuits have been translated to C programs and analyzed by software verifiers [20, 21, 22]. C programs can also be translated to SMV or BTOR2 models and verified by hardware model checkers [23, 24].

While MoXI-MC-FLOW can solve MoXI verification tasks by translating them to BTOR2 [12], the translation-based approach limits the expressiveness of the model-checking flow because verification problems cannot be precisely represented in BTOR2 if they involve more complex background theories, such as integer or real arithmetics. Moreover, to extend MoXI-MC-FLOW with new algorithms, tool developers need to dig into the BTOR2 model checkers.

1.2   Motivation to Develop MoXIchecker

To address the extensibility gap of the translation-based model-checking flow for MoXI, we implemented MoXIchecker, the first model checker that solves MoXI verification tasks directly without translating them to other intermediate languages. MoXIchecker takes as input a MoXI verification task, constructs the SMT formulas used to define the task, and implements its verification algorithms using the API of PySMT [25], a solver-agnostic Python library for SMT solvers. Currently, MoXIchecker supports the quantifier-free theories of bit-vectors, arrays, integers, and reals, and the implemented algorithms include BMC [26], k-induction [27], and IC3/PDR [28].

The benefits of MoXIchecker compared to MoXI-MC-Flow are threefold. First, MoXIchecker enjoys the complete expressiveness of SMT-LIB 2 and is applicable to verification tasks involving more complex background theories, as long as there exists an SMT solver supporting the used theory. In contrast, MoXI-MC-Flow is inadequate if the used theory is not representable in lower-level intermediate languages focusing on bit-vectors of fixed lengths and arrays. Second, MoXIchecker allows for convenient extension and fast prototyping of model-checking algorithms. To develop a new algorithm in MoXIchecker, one can simply work with the SMT formulas describing the model and manipulate them via the API of PySMT. In contrast, adding a new algorithm to the hardware model checkers used by MoXI-MC-Flow involves dealing with BTOR2 circuits. Moreover, MoXIchecker enables fair comparison of algorithms because the number of confounding variables (e.g., same parser, same SMT solver, same libraries) is kept to a minimum. Third, MoXIchecker has a robust frontend design because constructing SMT formulas that describe a MoXI verification task via PySMT is purely syntactical and less error-prone than translating the SMT formulas to BTOR2.

Furthermore, MoXIchecker is meant for use in education. It is an ideal framework for playing around with algorithms in course projects. The tool has a clean architecture and a slim code base.

Contributions. To sum up, our contributions in this paper include:

1. MoXIchecker, the first model checker that verifies MoXI tasks directly,
2. implemented as an extensible framework to accommodate various background theories and facilitate the development of algorithms for MoXI,
3. MoXIchecker's first three algorithms, BMC, k-induction, and IC3/PDR, and
4. an evaluation of MoXIchecker with MoXI-MC-Flow on about 400 MoXI verification tasks.

In our experiments, MoXIchecker solved a similar number of bit-vector tasks as MoXI-MC-Flow, which used highly-optimized BTOR2 model checkers as backend. Moreover, MoXIchecker was able to uniquely solve tasks using real arithmetics, which MoXI-MC-Flow cannot handle. These contributions are significant and novel because MoXIchecker supports the standardization of symbolic model checking around MoXI and provides an extensible framework for open-source implementations of verification algorithms for MoXI.

2   Background

In this section, we provide background knowledge for symbolic model checking and the intermediate verification language MoXI.

2.1   Symbolic Model Checking

The problem of symbolic model checking [1, 2] is to decide whether a model, usually represented as a *state-transition system* [29, 30], satisfies a specification. A state-transition system $\mathcal{M}$ can be described by an *initial condition* $I(s)$, a *transition condition* $T(s, s')$, and an *invariance condition* $Inv(s)$, where s and s' range over possible states of $\mathcal{M}$. Condition $I(s)$ evaluates to $\top$ if state s is an initial state of $\mathcal{M}$, and $T(s, s')$ evaluates to $\top$ if state s can transit to state s' via one step in $\mathcal{M}$ (we use $\top$ for *true*). A state $\hat{s}$ is *reachable* if $I(\hat{s})$ evaluates to $\top$ or $I(s_0) \wedge T(s_0, s_1) \wedge \ldots \wedge T(s_{k-1}, \hat{s})$ is satisfiable for some $k \geq 1$. Condition $Inv(s)$ is a constraint imposed on all reachable states in $\mathcal{M}$ (a reachable state that violates Inv is excluded for analysis).

A specification φ can be represented by a formula in linear temporal logic (LTL) [31], which is evaluated over the execution traces of a state-transition system. In the following, we refer to the tuple $(\mathcal{M}, \varphi)$ as a *verification task*, which asks if state-transition system $\mathcal{M}$ satisfies specification φ. *Reachability safety* is an essential category of specifications, inspecting the reachability of some target states marked by a *reachable condition* $Q(s)$. A reachability-safety verification task is described by the tuple (I, T, Inv, Q), where I, T, and Inv define a state-transition system $\mathcal{M}$ and Q defines an LTL formula "**always** $\neg Q$" as a specification φ for $\mathcal{M}$. A reachability-safety verification task is *safe* (resp. *unsafe*) if the target states are unreachable (resp. reachable).

In the research community of hardware model checking, verification tasks of sequential circuits can be encoded by the word-level language BTOR2 [13].

2.2   The Intermediate Verification Language MoXI

MoXI [3] extends the SMT-LIB 2 [7] format with constructs to describe verification tasks. Inheriting the expressiveness of SMT-LIB 2, MoXI offers a variety of background theories, ranging from bit-vectors and arrays (`QF_BV` and `QF_ABV`) to linear and nonlinear arithmetics over integers and reals (`QF_LIA`, `QF_LRA`, `QF_-NIA`, and `QF_NRA`), to represent models of hardware, software, and cyber-physical systems. As for specifications, MoXI supports reachability-safety queries with fairness constraints. We refer interested readers to the language design of MoXI [3] for more details. In the following, we use an example to show how a verification task is represented in MoXI.

Figure 1 shows a verification task of a three-bit counter in MoXI. Line 1 sets the background theory to `QF_BV`, which allows for quantifier-free formulas over the theory of bit-vectors with fixed sizes. Lines 2 to 8 define the behavior of the three-bit counter with command **define-system** and name the counter **main**. Counter **main** has an output variable s, which is a bit-vector of length three (attribute :output in line 4). Counter **main** has no inputs or local variables (attributes :input in line 3 and :local in line 5, respectively).

The initial condition in line 6 (attribute :init) initializes output s of counter main to #b000. The transition condition in line 7 (attribute :trans) increments the value of s by #b010 in each step. Note that a primed variable is treated as the next-state variable of its unprimed counterpart by MoXI. That is, s' holds the value of s after one step. The invariance condition in line 8 (attribute :inv) imposes true as a constraint on all reachable states of counter main. The specification for counter main is described by command check-system. The reachability condition rch_1 in line 13 (attribute :reachable) states that the value

```
1   (set-logic QF_BV)
2   (define-system main
3     :input ()
4     :output ((s (_ BitVec 3)))
5     :local ()
6     :init (= s #b000)
7     :trans (= s' (bvadd s #b010))
8     :inv true)
9   (check-system main
10    :input ()
11    :output ((s (_ BitVec 3)))
12    :local ()
13    :reachable (rch_1
             (= (bvurem s #b010) #b001))
14    :query (qry_rch_1 (rch_1)))
```

Fig. 1: An example verification task in MoXI

of s is an odd number, i.e., the remainder of s divided by #b010 equals #b001. Line 14 poses a query qry_rch_1 (attribute :query) to examine whether the LTL formula "always ¬rch_1" is satisfied by all execution traces of counter main.

The MoXI tool suite [12] provides an alternative representation of MoXI verification tasks in JSON format to facilitate tool development and information exchange. Figure 2 shows the corresponding JSON file for the verification task in Fig. 1. Our tool MoXIchecker takes MoXI verification tasks in JSON format as input. For details of the JSON representation, we refer interested readers to the MoXI JSON schema[1] in the MoXI tool suite.

To analyze a MoXI verification task, the model checker MoXI-MC-Flow in the MoXI tool suite translates the MoXI task to an equisatisfiable Btor2 verification task and invokes hardware model checkers for Btor2, e.g., AVR [14], BtorMC [13], and Pono [15], from the Hardware Model Checking Competitions [32].

3   Software Architecture of MoXIchecker

Figure 3 shows the software architecture of MoXIchecker, the first model checker for MoXI without translating verification tasks to lower-level languages. Implemented in the programming language Python, MoXIchecker is open-source on GitLab[2] and released under the Apache License 2.0. On a MoXI verification task in JSON format, MoXIchecker uses the standard JSON package of Python to load the input file and constructs SMT formulas for the initial, transition, invariance, and reachable conditions by calling the API of the solver-agnostic library PySMT [25] for SMT solvers. It then performs model checking on the reachability-safety verification task (I, T, Inv, Q). The output of MoXIchecker on a MoXI verification task is a verdict to indicate whether the task is safe or unsafe.

Different from MoXI-MC-Flow in the MoXI tool suite [12], which translates verification tasks in MoXI to Btor2 [13] and invokes hardware model checkers,

---
[1] https://github.com/ModelChecker/moxi-mc-flow/tree/main/json-schema
[2] https://gitlab.com/sosy-lab/software/moxichecker

```
1   [ { "command": "set-logic", "logic": "QF_BV" },
2     { "command": "define-system",
3       "symbol": "main",
4       "input": [],
5       "output": [{
6           "symbol": "s",
7           "sort": { "identifier": { "symbol": "BitVec", "indices": [3] }}}],
8       "local": [],
9       "init": {
10          "identifier": { "symbol": "=", "indices": [] },
11          "args": [{ "identifier": "s" }, { "identifier": "#b000" }]},
12      "trans": {
13          "identifier": { "symbol": "=", "indices": [] },
14          "args": [
15            { "identifier": "s'" },
16            {"identifier": { "symbol": "bvadd", "indices": [] },
17             "args": [{ "identifier": "s" }, { "identifier": "#b010" }]}]},
18      "inv": { "identifier": "true" }},
19    { "command": "check-system",
20      "symbol": "main",
21      "input": [],
22      "output": [{
23          "symbol": "s",
24          "sort": { "identifier": { "symbol": "BitVec", "indices": [3] }}}],
25      "local": [],
26      "reachable": [
27          { "symbol": "rch_1",
28            "formula": { "identifier": { "symbol": "=", "indices": [] },
29            "args": [
30              {"identifier": { "symbol": "bvurem", "indices": [] },
31               "args": [{ "identifier": "s" }, { "identifier": "#b010" }]},
32              { "identifier": "#b001" }]}}],
33      "query": [{ "symbol": "qry_rch_1", "formulas": ["rch_1"] }]}]
```

Fig. 2: A JSON representation of the MoXI verification task in Fig. 1

MoXICHECKER implements its model-checking engines using the API of PySMT. Currently, MoXICHECKER supports QF_BV, QF_ABV, QF_LIA, QF_LRA, QF_NIA, and QF_NRA as the background theory. The elegant software architecture of MoXI-CHECKER facilitates the addition of new background theories and yields a slim code base (about 700 lines in release 0.2).

We adapted and integrated the implementations of BMC [26], k-induction [27], and IC3/PDR [28] in PySMT[3] into our framework. In addition, we demonstrate the extensibility of MoXICHECKER by contributing a k-induction implementation that takes advantage of incremental solving of SMT solvers by reusing solver stacks. Compared to the non-incremental version in PySMT, the incremental k-induction was more efficient and solved more tasks in the evaluation.

3.1   Example

We demonstrate the working of MoXICHECKER by invoking it on the verification task in Fig. 1. MoXICHECKER consumes the JSON file of the MoXI verification task in Fig. 2 as input and constructs SMT formulas $s = 0$, $s' = s + 2$, $\top$, and $s\%2 = 1$,

---

[3] https://github.com/pysmt/pysmt/blob/master/examples/model_checking.py

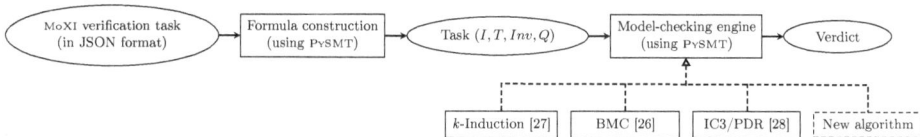

Fig. 3: Software architecture of MoXIchecker

as the initial, transition, invariance, and reachability conditions, respectively. Note that variable s is a bit-vector of length three, and variable s' is its next-state counterpart. To honor the invariance condition, MoXIchecker conjoins it with initial and transition conditions, respectively. As the invariance condition is $\top$ in the example verification task, we omit it in the following explanation.

To solve the verification task, MoXIchecker considers "$\textbf{always } \neg(s\%2 = 1)$" as the specification for the state-transition system. By applying k-induction [27], MoXIchecker shows that both the *base case* $(s = 0) \Rightarrow \neg(s\%2 = 1)$ and the *step case* $\neg(s\%2 = 1) \wedge (s' = s + 1) \Rightarrow \neg(s'\%2 = 1)$ for $k = 1$ hold. Therefore, MoXIchecker concludes that counter `main` in Fig. 1 satisfies its specification.

3.2 Discussion

In the following, we discuss the ongoing development progress of MoXIchecker, the differences between MoXIchecker and a related model-checking framework PyVMT [33], and the trade-offs of using the programming language Python.

The current version of MoXIchecker (release 0.2) misses the support for creating subsystems (via attribute `:subsys` in command `define-system`), a key feature of MoXI to compose multiple state-transition systems. MoXIchecker also needs further enhancement to handle fairness constraints (via attribute `:fairness` in command `check-system`) and background theories with quantifiers. Compared to MoXI-MC-Flow, which has not yet supported quantifiers, supporting quantifiers in MoXIchecker is straightforward because it is not limited by lower-level modeling languages like Btor2. In addition, MoXI defines a format for *verification witnesses* [34, 35], e.g., an error trace if the specification is violated or an invariant if the specification is satisfied. We are actively extending the language support of MoXIchecker to cover all features of MoXI.

PyVMT [33] is a Python library to construct and verify transition systems specified in the language VMT [8]. It offers API functions to read and construct a VMT model, and verifies the model by invoking backend model-checking engines (e.g., nuxmv [36] or IC3ia [37]). In contrast, MoXIchecker is a standalone tool that consumes a MoXI model as input and implements its verification algorithms without calling external model checkers. Moreover, MoXIchecker has the potential for modular verification because MoXI supports constructing bigger systems with smaller subsystems, while VMT only allows flattened transition systems.

Finally, using Python to implement MoXIchecker simplifies the development process thanks to the convenient language features of Python. It makes MoXIchecker ideal for introducing students to model checking. While using Python may limit the efficiency of the tool (especially when a model-checking approach also requires time-consuming operations outside SMT solving), mature acceleration approaches for Python, e.g., writing the time-consuming parts in Cython and compiling into C code, can be applied to mitigate the performance issue.

4   Evaluation

To demonstrate the performance and extensibility of MoXIchecker, we compared it to MoXI-MC-Flow, the translation-based model checker for MoXI [12], which invokes hardware model checkers for Btor2 as backend. Our experiments aim to answer the following research questions:

- RQ1: Is MoXIchecker effective and efficient compared to MoXI-MC-Flow on QF_BV and QF_ABV tasks?
- RQ2: Can MoXIchecker solve tasks using more complex background theories, which MoXI-MC-Flow cannot solve?

4.1   Experimental Setup

We evaluated MoXIchecker and MoXI-MC-Flow on two sets of MoXI verification tasks in JSON format. The first benchmark set consists of 412 QF_BV tasks (247 safe and 165 unsafe) and 41 QF_ABV tasks (28 safe and 13 unsafe), all sourced from the MoXI tool suite [12]. Due to the lack of publicly available verification tasks involving more complex theories, we handcrafted 9 tasks using the theories of QF_LIA, QF_LRA, QF_NIA, and QF_NRA to test the support for more complex theories of MoXIchecker.

We used MoXIchecker version 0.2 and MoXI-MC-Flow at commit 52f720b1 in the experiments. MoXIchecker called SMT solvers Z3 [38] and MathSAT5 [39] for QF_BV, QF_ABV, QF_LIA, and QF_LRA tasks; for tasks using nonlinear arithmetics, MoXIchecker employed Z3. MoXI-MC-Flow invoked Btor2 model checkers AVR [14] and Pono [15] to solve QF_BV and QF_ABV and tasks. AVR and Pono used Yices2 [40] and Boolector3 [13] as their backend SMT solvers, respectively. QF_LIA and QF_NIA tasks were also solved by Btor2 model checkers through encoding integers as 32-bit bit-vectors. The version of MoXI-MC-Flow used in our evaluation had no support for reals. Both MoXIchecker and MoXI-MC-Flow used k-induction for verification. (For MoXI-MC-Flow, AVR and Pono were configured to use k-induction on translated Btor2 tasks.)

All experiments were conducted on machines running the GNU/Linux operating system (x86_64-linux, Ubuntu 22.04 with Linux kernel 5.15), each equipped with 33 GB of RAM and a 3.4 GHz Intel Xeon E3-1230 v5 CPU with 8 processing units. Each task was limited to 2 CPU cores, 15 min of CPU time, and 15 GB of RAM. We used BenchExec [41] to ensure reliable resource measurement and reproducible results.

4.2   Experimental Results

RQ1: Performance of MoXIchecker. Table 1 summarizes the experimental results of MoXIchecker and MoXI-MC-Flow on 412 QF_BV and 41 QF_ABV verification tasks. MoXIchecker, when using MathSAT5 as the backend solver

Table 1: Summary of verification results on 453 `QF_BV` and `QF_ABV` tasks

Tool	MoXIchecker				MoXI-MC-Flow	
Backend	MathSAT	MathSAT^{incr}	Z3	Z3^{incr}	AVR	Pono
Correct results	217	**222**	212	217	221	221
`QF_BV`	190	195	195	**200**	193	193
Proofs	54	56	56	**57**	54	56
Alarms	136	139	139	**143**	139	137
`QF_ABV`	27	27	17	17	**28**	**28**
Proofs	15	15	15	15	15	15
Alarms	12	12	2	2	**13**	**13**
Errors and Unknown	236	231	241	236	232	232

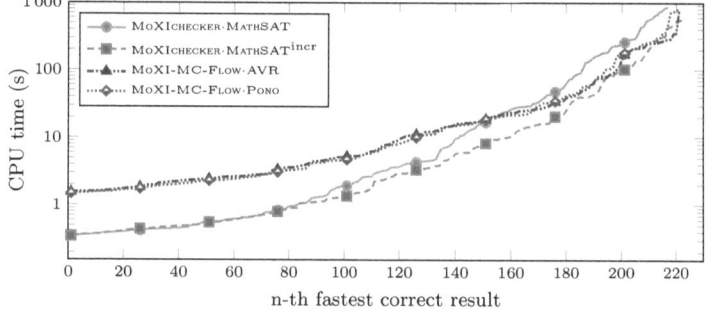

Fig. 4: MoXIchecker vs. MoXI-MC-Flow on 453 `QF_BV` and `QF_ABV` tasks

and incremental solving, delivered the most correct results. Notably, MoXIchecker solved 17 tasks that MoXI-MC-Flow failed to translate to Btor2.

Despite being implemented in Python, MoXIchecker demonstrated a comparable performance to MoXI-MC-Flow, which employs highly-optimized hardware model checkers written in C++ as backend. This is mainly because the bottleneck of SMT-based verification algorithms lies in solving SMT formulas. A preliminary run-time profiling for MoXIchecker by cProfile showed that solving formulas accounted for more than 90 % of the run-time for the more time-consuming tasks. The results suggest that using Python to construct and manipulate SMT formulas does not incur much overhead for MoXIchecker.

In our evaluation, MoXIchecker was also more efficient than MoXI-MC-Flow in terms of CPU-time consumption. Figure 4 shows a quantile plot comparing MoXIchecker and MoXI-MC-Flow on the `QF_BV` tasks. A data point (x, y) in the plot indicates that there are x tasks, each of which can be correctly solved by the respective tool within a time bound y seconds. The figure shows that MoXIchecker ran faster than MoXI-MC-Flow, especially for tasks that can be solved quickly, because MoXI-MC-Flow had a slower startup time due to its translation process (note the higher y-intercept of roughly 3 s in Fig. 4).

Figure 5 shows a head-to-head comparison of MoXIchecker (cf. ■ in Fig. 4) and MoXI-MC-Flow (cf. ▲ in Fig. 4) in a scatter plot. A data point (x, y) in the plot represents a task that was solved by both MoXI-MC-Flow and

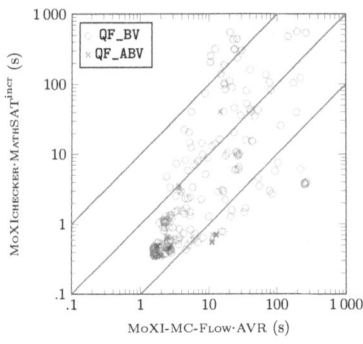 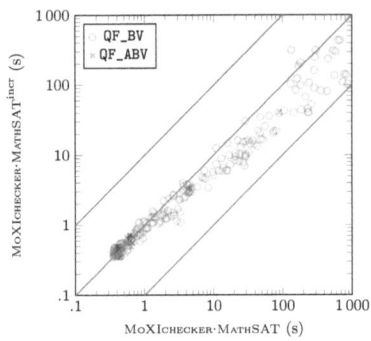

Fig. 5: Efficiency of MoXIchecker vs. MoXI-MC-Flow on QF_BV and QF_ABV tasks

Fig. 6: Effect of incremental SMT solving in MoXIchecker on QF_BV and QF_ABV tasks

MoXIchecker, for which the former took x seconds, while the latter took y seconds. The figure shows that the efficiency of MoXIchecker was competitive against MoXI-MC-Flow. In particular, out of the 205 tasks solved by both, MoXIchecker was faster than MoXI-MC-Flow on 156 tasks.

In addition to the comparison with MoXI-MC-Flow, we evaluated the impact of backend solvers and incremental solving on MoXIchecker. From Table 1, observe that MathSAT5 and Z3 delivered similar performance, with the former being slightly more effective. In contrast, incremental SMT solving had a more pronounced effect on both the effectiveness and efficiency of MoXI-checker. The performance improvement of our k-induction implementation (MoXIchecker·MathSAT^{incr}) over the implementation provided by PySMT (MoXIchecker·MathSAT) is also evident in Fig. 4 and Fig. 6.

RQ2: Extensibility of MoXIchecker. Table 2 lists the results of MoXI-checker and MoXI-MC-Flow on 9 handcrafted model-checking problems involving integer and real arithmetics. MoXIchecker correctly solved all tasks. In contrast, MoXI-MC-Flow produced wrong results or timeouts for the tasks containing integers (upper half of Table 2) and had no support for tasks containing reals (lower half of Table 2). Unlike MoXIchecker, which utilized Z3 and thus supported the theories over integers and reals, MoXI-MC-Flow approximated integers with bit-vectors (of length 32 by default). Due to the potential issues of overflow and underflow in bit-vector arithmetics, such approximation is both *unsound* and *incomplete*, therefore causing the incorrect verification results in Table 2. This illustrative experiment shows that, compared to MoXI-MC-Flow, MoXIchecker is (1) more reliable, as it does not yield wrong results due to approximation, and (2) more versatile, as it supports many background theories.

5   Conclusion

We introduced MoXIchecker, the first model checker for MoXI that performs model checking with the SMT formulas describing a MoXI task directly. Compared to MoXI-MC-Flow [12], which translates verification tasks to Btor2 [13] and invokes hardware model checkers, MoXIchecker accommodates MoXI verification

Table 2: MoXIchecker vs. MoXI-MC-Flow on tasks using integers and reals

Task	Theory	Verdict	MoXIchecker	MoXI-MC-Flow
FibonacciSequence	QF_LIA	safe	safe	unsafe
IntIncrement	QF_LIA	unsafe	unsafe	safe
IntCounter	QF_LIA	safe	safe	timeout
IntMultiply	QF_NIA	safe	safe	unsafe
BoundedLinearGrowth	QF_LRA	safe	safe	unsupported
DoubleDelay2	QF_LRA	unsafe	unsafe	unsupported
OscillatingRatio	QF_NRA	safe	safe	unsupported
SafeNonlinearGrowth	QF_NRA	safe	safe	unsupported
NonlinearGrowth	QF_NRA	unsafe	unsafe	unsupported

tasks with various background theories, facilitates the implementation of new model-checking algorithms, abstracts from specific SMT solvers using the API of PySMT, and has a robust frontend design that avoids potential translation bugs. Currently, MoXIchecker supports the quantifier-free theories of bit-vectors, arrays, integers, and reals, and implements BMC [26], k-induction [27], and IC3/PDR [28] for verification. In our evaluation, MoXIchecker achieved a comparable performance against MoXI-MC-Flow on bit-vector tasks and uniquely solved tasks using integer or real arithmetics. We envision MoXIchecker to facilitate open-source implementations for model-checking techniques around MoXI and become a cornerstone for wider adoption of symbolic model checking. For future work, we will enhance the language support of MoXIchecker, improve the existing verification algorithms and implement new ones, and apply MoXIchecker to software programs or cyber-physical systems. In particular, we want to implement algorithms using Craig interpolation [42] for MoXI. Several interpolation-based algorithms [43, 44, 45] for hardware model checking have been transferred to software verification and demonstrated competitive performance [5, 6].

Data-Availability Statement. The MoXIchecker release 0.2 is available at Zenodo [46] and at `https://gitlab.com/sosy-lab/software/moxichecker`. Additional supplementary materials for this article, including the reproduction information and interactive HTML tables for convenient browsing of the evaluation results, are available at `https://www.sosy-lab.org/research/moxichecker/`.

Funding Statement. This project was funded in part by the Deutsche Forschungsgemeinschaft (DFG) – 378803395 (ConVeY) and 536040111 (Bridge).

References

1. Burch, J.R., Clarke, E.M., McMillan, K.L., Dill, D.L., Hwang, L.J.: Symbolic model checking: 10^{20} states and beyond. In: Proc. LICS. pp. 428–439. IEEE (1990). `https://doi.org/10.1109/LICS.1990.113767`
2. McMillan, K.L.: Symbolic Model Checking. Springer (1993). `https://doi.org/10.1007/978-1-4615-3190-6`

3. Rozier, K.Y., Dureja, R., Irfan, A., Johannsen, C., Nukala, K., Shankar, N., Tinelli, C., Vardi, M.Y.: MoXI: An intermediate language for symbolic model checking. In: Proc. SPIN. pp. 26–46. LNCS 14624, Springer (2024). https://doi.org/10.1007/978-3-031-66149-5_2

4. Beyer, D., Wehrheim, H.: Verification artifacts in cooperative verification: Survey and unifying component framework. In: Proc. ISoLA (1). pp. 143–167. LNCS 12476, Springer (2020). https://doi.org/10.1007/978-3-030-61362-4_8

5. Beyer, D., Lee, N.Z., Wendler, P.: Interpolation and SAT-based model checking revisited: Adoption to software verification. J. Autom. Reasoning (2024). https://doi.org/10.1007/s10817-024-09702-9

6. Beyer, D., Chien, P.C., Jankola, M., Lee, N.Z.: A transferability study of interpolation-based hardware model checking for software verification. Proc. ACM Softw. Eng. 1(FSE) (2024). https://doi.org/10.1145/3660797

7. Barrett, C., Stump, A., Tinelli, C.: The SMT-LIB Standard: Version 2.0. Tech. rep., University of Iowa (2010), https://smtlib.cs.uiowa.edu/papers/smt-lib-reference-v2.0-r10.12.21.pdf

8. Cimatti, A., Griggio, A., Tonetta, S.: The VMT-LIB language and tools. In: Proc. SMT. CEUR Workshop Proceedings, vol. 3185, pp. 80–89. CEUR-WS.org (2022). https://ceur-ws.org/Vol-3185/extended9547.pdf

9. McMillan, K.L.: The SMV system. In: Symbolic Model Checking, pp. 61–85 (1993). https://doi.org/10.1007/978-1-4615-3190-6_4

10. DeLine, R., Leino, R.: BoogiePL: A typed procedural language for checking object-oriented programs. Tech. Rep. MSR-TR-2005-70, Microsoft Research (2005). https://www.microsoft.com/en-us/research/publication/boogiepl-a-typed-procedural-language-for-checking-object-oriented-programs/

11. Beyer, D., Lee, N.Z.: The transformation game: Joining forces for verification. In: Principles of Verification: Cycling the Probabilistic Landscape. pp. 175–205. LNCS 15262, Springer (2024). https://doi.org/10.1007/978-3-031-75778-5_9

12. Johannsen, C., Nukala, K., Dureja, R., Irfan, A., Shankar, N., Tinelli, C., Vardi, M.Y., Rozier, K.Y.: The MoXI model exchange tool suite. In: Proc. CAV. pp. 203–218. LNCS 14681, Springer (2024). https://doi.org/10.1007/978-3-031-65627-9_10

13. Niemetz, A., Preiner, M., Wolf, C., Biere, A.: Btor2, BtorMC, and Boolector 3.0. In: Proc. CAV. pp. 587–595. LNCS 10981, Springer (2018). https://doi.org/10.1007/978-3-319-96145-3_32

14. Goel, A., Sakallah, K.: AVR: Abstractly verifying reachability. In: Proc. TACAS. pp. 413–422. LNCS 12078, Springer (2020). https://doi.org/10.1007/978-3-030-45190-5_23

15. Mann, M., Irfan, A., Lonsing, F., Yang, Y., Zhang, H., Brown, K., Gupta, A., Barrett, C.W.: Pono: A flexible and extensible SMT-based model checker. In: Proc. CAV. pp. 461–474. LNCS 12760, Springer (2021). https://doi.org/10.1007/978-3-030-81688-9_22

16. IEEE standard for Verilog hardware description language (2006). https://doi.org/10.1109/IEEESTD.2006.99495

17. Minhas, M., Hasan, O., Saghar, K.: Ver2Smv: A tool for automatic Verilog to SMV translation for verifying digital circuits. In: Proc. ICEET. pp. 1–5 (2018). https://doi.org/10.1109/ICEET1.2018.8338617

18. Irfan, A., Cimatti, A., Griggio, A., Roveri, M., Sebastiani, R.: Verilog2SMV: A tool for word-level verification. In: Proc. DATE. pp. 1156–1159 (2016), https://ieeexplore.ieee.org/document/7459485

19. Mukherjee, R., Tautschnig, M., Kroening, D.: v2c: A Verilog to C translator. In: Proc. TACAS. pp. 580–586. LNCS 9636, Springer (2016). https://doi.org/10.1007/978-3-662-49674-9_38

20. Beyer, D., Chien, P.C., Lee, N.Z.: Bridging hardware and software analysis with Btor2C: A word-level-circuit-to-C translator. In: Proc. TACAS (2). pp. 152–172. LNCS 13994, Springer (2023). https://doi.org/10.1007/978-3-031-30820-8_12

21. Ádám, Z., Beyer, D., Chien, P.C., Lee, N.Z., Sirrenberg, N.: Btor2-Cert: A certifying hardware-verification framework using software analyzers. In: Proc. TACAS (3). pp. 129–149. LNCS 14572, Springer (2024). https://doi.org/10.1007/978-3-031-57256-2_7

22. Tafese, J., Garcia-Contreras, I., Gurfinkel, A.: Btor2MLIR: A format and toolchain for hardware verification. In: Proc. FMCAD. pp. 55–63. TU Wien Academic Press (2023). https://doi.org/10.34727/2023/ISBN.978-3-85448-060-0_13

23. Chien, P.C., Lee, N.Z.: CPV: A circuit-based program verifier (competition contribution). In: Proc. TACAS (3). pp. 365–370. LNCS 14572, Springer (2024). https://doi.org/10.1007/978-3-031-57256-2_22

24. Griggio, A., Jonáš, M.: Kratos2: An SMT-based model checker for imperative programs. In: Proc. CAV. pp. 423–436. Springer (2023). https://doi.org/10.1007/978-3-031-37709-9_20

25. Gario, M., Micheli, A.: PySMT: A solver-agnostic library for fast prototyping of SMT-based algorithms. In: Proc. SMT (2015)

26. Biere, A., Cimatti, A., Clarke, E.M., Zhu, Y.: Symbolic model checking without BDDs. In: Proc. TACAS. pp. 193–207. LNCS 1579, Springer (1999). https://doi.org/10.1007/3-540-49059-0_14

27. Sheeran, M., Singh, S., Stålmarck, G.: Checking safety properties using induction and a SAT-solver. In: Proc. FMCAD, pp. 127–144. LNCS 1954, Springer (2000). https://doi.org/10.1007/3-540-40922-X_8

28. Bradley, A.R.: SAT-based model checking without unrolling. In: Proc. VMCAI. pp. 70–87. LNCS 6538, Springer (2011). https://doi.org/10.1007/978-3-642-18275-4_7

29. Hughes, G.E., Cresswell, M.J.: A New Introduction to Modal Logic. Routledge (1996). https://www.worldcat.org/isbn/978-0-41512-600-7

30. Clarke, E.M., Henzinger, T.A., Veith, H., Bloem, R.: Handbook of Model Checking. Springer (2018). https://doi.org/10.1007/978-3-319-10575-8

31. Piterman, N., Pnueli, A.: Temporal logic and fair discrete systems. In: Handbook of Model Checking, pp. 27–73. Springer (2018). https://doi.org/10.1007/978-3-319-10575-8_2

32. Biere, A., van Dijk, T., Heljanko, K.: Hardware model-checking competition 2017. In: Proc. FMCAD. p. 9. IEEE (2017). https://doi.org/10.23919/FMCAD.2017.8102233

33. PyVMT: A Python library to interact with transition systems. https://github.com/pyvmt/pyvmt, accessed: 2024-10-08

34. Beyer, D., Dangl, M., Dietsch, D., Heizmann, M., Lemberger, T., Tautschnig, M.: Verification witnesses. ACM Trans. Softw. Eng. Methodol. 31(4), 57:1–57:69 (2022). https://doi.org/10.1145/3477579

35. McConnell, R.M., Mehlhorn, K., Näher, S., Schweitzer, P.: Certifying algorithms. Computer Science Review 5(2), 119–161 (2011). https://doi.org/10.1016/j.cosrev.2010.09.009

36. Cavada, R., Cimatti, A., Dorigatti, M., Griggio, A., Mariotti, A., Micheli, A., Mover, S., Roveri, M., Tonetta, S.: The NUXMV symbolic model checker. In: Proc. CAV. pp. 334–342. LNCS 8559, Springer (2014). https://doi.org/10.1007/978-3-319-08867-9_22

37. Cimatti, A., Griggio, A., Mover, S., Tonetta, S.: IC3 modulo theories via implicit predicate abstraction. In: Proc. TACAS. pp. 46–61. LNCS 8413, Springer (2014). https://doi.org/10.1007/978-3-642-54862-8_4

38. de Moura, L.M., Bjørner, N.: Z3: An efficient SMT solver. In: Proc. TACAS. pp. 337–340. LNCS 4963, Springer (2008). https://doi.org/10.1007/978-3-540-78800-3_24

39. Cimatti, A., Griggio, A., Schaafsma, B.J., Sebastiani, R.: The MATHSAT5 SMT solver. In: Proc. TACAS. pp. 93–107. LNCS 7795, Springer (2013). https://doi.org/10.1007/978-3-642-36742-7_7

40. Dutertre, B.: YICES 2.2. In: Proc. CAV. pp. 737–744. LNCS 8559, Springer (2014). https://doi.org/10.1007/978-3-319-08867-9_49

41. Beyer, D., Löwe, S., Wendler, P.: Reliable benchmarking: Requirements and solutions. Int. J. Softw. Tools Technol. Transfer **21**(1), 1–29 (2019). https://doi.org/10.1007/s10009-017-0469-y

42. Craig, W.: Linear reasoning. A new form of the Herbrand-Gentzen theorem. J. Symb. Log. **22**(3), 250–268 (1957). https://doi.org/10.2307/2963593

43. McMillan, K.L.: Interpolation and SAT-based model checking. In: Proc. CAV. pp. 1–13. LNCS 2725, Springer (2003). https://doi.org/10.1007/978-3-540-45069-6_1

44. Vizel, Y., Grumberg, O.: Interpolation-sequence based model checking. In: Proc. FMCAD. pp. 1–8. IEEE (2009). https://doi.org/10.1109/FMCAD.2009.5351148

45. Vizel, Y., Grumberg, O., Shoham, S.: Intertwined forward-backward reachability analysis using interpolants. In: Proc. TACAS. pp. 308–323. LNCS 7795, Springer (2013). https://doi.org/10.1007/978-3-642-36742-7_22

46. Ates, S., Beyer, D., Chien, P.C., Lee, N.Z.: MOXICHECKER release 0.2. Zenodo (2024). https://doi.org/10.5281/zenodo.13895872

Towards Verifying Security Policies
for Infinite-State Systems

Quentin Peyras[1,3]([✉])[iD], Ghada Gharbi[1]([✉])[iD], and Souheib Baarir[2][iD]

[1] LRE, EPITA, Le Kremlin-Bicêtre, France
ghada.gharbi@epita.fr
[2] LIP 6, Sorbonne University, Paris, France
souheib.baarir@lip6.fr
[3] IRIT CNRS UPS, Université de Toulouse, Toulouse, France
quentin.peyras@irit.fr

Abstract. Non-interference ensures no unauthorized data leaks during system execution. Verifying security policies is complex, requiring analysis of multiple execution paths. Hyperproperties provide a framework to describe security policies like non-interference. However, existing methods like HyperLTL are limited to finite-state models. This paper introduces a case study illustrating the use of HyperFOLTL, designed for infinite-state systems, and presents a formal approach to verify security policies in such systems.

Keywords: Non-Interference · Hyperproperties · HyperFOLTL · First-Order Logic · Distributed Systems

1 Introduction

Distributed systems are crucial in modern computing, where security is vital for data integrity and privacy. Mechanisms such as non-interference and confidentiality policies are key defenses against potential threats. To ensure system correctness and security, formal methods are often used. While safety and liveness can be expressed using temporal logics like LTL [25], security policies require comparing multiple executions, leading to the introduction of HyperLTL for specifying hyperproperties. However, the complexity of distributed systems, with their dynamic interactions, necessitates more expressive logics. HyperFOLTL extends HyperLTL [6] with First-Order (FO) quantifiers, enabling the specification of hyperproperties in infinite-state systems.

In this paper, we propose to use HyperFOLTL logic as a potential solution for expressing security policies and a formal definition of security policy satisfiability problem, defined in terms of HyperFOLTL formulas. The paper is organized as follows. Section 2 introduces a case stydy, the leader election protocol. Section 3 outlines temporal logics for expressing hyperproperties. Section 4 details our approach. We will study the formal proof of security property's satisfiability (i.e., non-interference). The proof is conducted on the case study. Section 5 formally

J. Protzenko and A. Raad (Eds.): VSTTE 2024, LNCS 15525, pp. 15–27, 2025.
https://doi.org/10.1007/978-3-031-86695-1_2

defines the concept of a linking invariant, used to reason about multiple system traces. Section 6 describes related works and finally we will conclude and give future works.

2   Problem Statement

Non-interference, first introduced by Goguen and Meseguer [17], is a key security property in distributed systems, ensuring data integrity and confidentiality across different security domains. It prevents sensitive information from leaking to unauthorized users or processes.

Leader Election Protocol. Let's explore a motivating example that demonstrates a non-interference security property in the context of a distributed system: the leader election protocol [4]. This will showcase our approach and highlight the challenges of verifying security policies.

The leader election protocol operates in a unidirectional ring network, where each node communicates with its neighbor in one direction. The goal is to elect the node with the largest identifier as the leader. Each node maintains a list of identifiers (represented by **msgs**), initially containing only its own, and asynchronously sends its identifier to its successor, adding any larger identifiers to the list. A node becomes the leader if it receives its own identifier back.

Key assumptions include asynchronous message transmission, a reliable network with no data loss, and the tolerance of transmission delays. Node identifiers are integers, allowing for total ordering, simplifying comparisons during the election process. It is important to note that the example being analyzed is modeled as an infinite-state system solely based on the number of nodes it comprises.

A key security concern arises from the assumption that an attacker can observe message sequences without accessing their content. This raises the question of whether the attacker can deduce the leader's identity through message patterns alone. Given the leader's pivotal role in decision-making and resource control, such disclosure could have serious consequences in distributed systems like distributed databases and file systems, or cloud services.

3   Formalizing Hyperproperties

In this section, we present the formalism of hyperproperties.

3.1   For Finite-State Systems

In this part, we consider the formalism of labeled transition systems, a standard method for modeling distributed systems [2,16,17,27]. Labeled transition systems allows the specification of safety and liveness properties using temporal logics such as Linear Temporal Logic (LTL). However, when it comes to reasoning about security policies, a more sophisticated class of properties, known as hyperproperties, is necessary. Unlike trace properties, expressible in LTL, and branching properties, expressible in CTL, hyperproperties requires the comparison and linkage of multiple distinct traces. The primary logic used to specify hyperproperties is HyperLTL [5,6], achieved by extending LTL with path quantifiers that bind each atomic proposition (the set of atomic propositions is denoted as **AP**) to a specific trace. This extension allows for the comparison of traces by connecting atomic propositions across different paths using LTL operators.

Definition 1 (HyperLTL - Syntax). *HyperLTL formulas are defined by the grammar :*

- $\psi ::= \phi \mid \exists \pi \cdot \psi \mid \forall \pi \cdot \psi$
- $\phi ::= a_\pi (a \in \mathbf{AP}) \mid \neg\phi \mid \phi \vee \phi \mid \mathbf{X}\phi \mid \phi \,\mathbf{U}\, \phi$

We can define the semantics of HyperLTL in a manner similar to that of LTL. However, it is essential to take into account a set of potential traces for path quantifiers.

Definition 2 (HyperLTL - Semantics). *Let T be a set of traces, Π a set of trace variables and $\mathcal{C}_\Pi : \Pi \to T$ a partial assignment of those variables. $\mathcal{C}_\Pi[\pi \mapsto t']$ denotes the assignment equals to $\mathcal{C}_\Pi$ everywhere but for π that is mapped to t'.*

- $T, \mathcal{C}_\Pi, n \vDash \exists \pi \cdot \psi$ *iif there exists* $t' \in T$ *such that* $T, \mathcal{C}_\Pi[\pi \mapsto t'], n \vDash \psi$
- $T, \mathcal{C}_\Pi, n \vDash \forall \pi \cdot \psi$ *iif for all* $t' \in T$ *we have* $T, \mathcal{C}_\Pi[\pi \mapsto t'], n \vDash \psi$
- $T, \mathcal{C}_\Pi, n \vDash a_\pi$ *iif* $a \in \mathcal{C}_\Pi(\pi)(n)$
- *other connectives follow the inductive definition of LTL semantics*
- $T, \mathcal{C}_\Pi, n \vDash \psi_1 \vee \psi_2$ *iif* $T, \mathcal{C}_\Pi, n \vDash \psi_1$ *or* $T, \mathcal{C}_\Pi, n \vDash \psi_2$
- $T, \mathcal{C}_\Pi, n \vDash \mathbf{X}\psi$ *iif* $T, \mathcal{C}_\Pi, n+1 \vDash \psi$
- $T, \mathcal{C}_\Pi, n \vDash \psi_1 \,\mathbf{U}\, \psi_2$ *iif there exist* $i \geq n$ *such that* $T, \mathcal{C}_\Pi, i \vDash \psi_2$ *and for all* $n \leq j < i, T, \mathcal{C}_\Pi, j \vDash \psi_1$

The general **HyperLTL** satisfiability problem is undecidable. Nevertheless, it is possible to define a specific fragment of **HyperLTL**, called **HyperLTL$_2$** , that is both decidable and capable of expressing all the relevant security policies as discussed in [5].

3.2   Generalization to Infinite-State Systems

When specifying concurrent and infinite-state systems, our emphasis lies in defining initial states and transitions using first-order logic. This approach, which is standard for specifying and verifying such systems [7, 18–20, 23, 24], necessitates augmenting first-order logic with a unique prime operator. This operator enables referencing the values of relations after a transition has been executed.

Definition 3 (Prime operator). *If r is a relation symbol, r' represents the value of r at the subsequent time instant (using LTL notation, $r'(\boldsymbol{x}) \equiv \mathbf{X}(r(\boldsymbol{x}))$). For a signature Σ, the signature of the primed relations and functions derived from this Σ is denoted as Σ'.*

Furthermore, a primed first-order (FO) formula on Σ refers to an FO formula on the signature $\Sigma \cup \Sigma'$. Such a formula is interpreted using a pair (m, m') of FO structures over Σ : one interprets the non-primed symbols, and the other interprets the primed symbols, thus defining the temporal evolution of the system between two successive states. If this interpretation satisfies the formula ϕ, we denote it as $m, m' \vDash \phi$.

Then, systems can be specified using FO formulas [22].

Definition 4 (FO transition systems). *A FO transition system is a tuple $\mathbf{Spec} = (\Sigma, \iota, \tau)$ where: Σ is an FO signature; ι is an FO formula defining initials states; τ is a primed FO formula defining possible transitions. Let t be a sequence of FO structures sharing the same domain D, we say that t is a trace of $\mathbf{Spec}$ if $t_0 \vDash \iota$ and $\forall i \in \mathbb{N}$ we have $t_i, t_{i+1} \vDash \tau$.*

Now that systems can be specified, a logic for reasoning about them is required. However, **HyperLTL** only supports finite-state systems. To handle infinite-state systems, one solution is to extend **HyperLTL** with FO quantifiers [10,12,13], leading to HyperFOLTL.

Definition 5 (HyperFOLTL). *HyperFOLTL syntax is given by adding FO quantifiers to the syntax of **HyperLTL**, the syntax of a HyperFOLTL formula ψ follows the grammar:*

- $\psi ::= \phi \mid \exists \pi \cdot \psi \mid \forall \pi \cdot \psi;$
- $\phi ::= r_\pi(\boldsymbol{x})^1 \; (r \in \Sigma) \mid \neg\phi \mid \phi \vee \phi \mid \mathbf{X}\phi \mid \phi \, \mathbf{U} \, \phi \mid \forall x \cdot \phi.$

Let T be a set of traces sharing the same domain D, Π a set of trace variables, $\mathcal{C}_\Pi : \Pi \rightharpoonup T$ a partial assignment of those variables to FO traces, $\mathcal{V}$ a set of variables and $\mathcal{C}$ an assignment of those variables. The semantics of ψ over T is defined as follows:

- $D, T, \mathcal{C}_\Pi, \mathcal{C}, n \vDash \forall \pi \cdot \psi$ *iff for all $t' \in T$ we have $D, T, \mathcal{C}_\Pi[\pi \mapsto t'], \mathcal{C}, n \vDash \psi;$*
- $D, T, \mathcal{C}_\Pi, \mathcal{C}, n \vDash r_\pi(\boldsymbol{x})$ *iff $\mathcal{C}_\Pi(\pi)$ satisfies $r(\boldsymbol{x})$ with assignment $\mathcal{C};$*
- $D, T, \mathcal{C}_\Pi, \mathcal{C}, n \vDash \forall x \cdot \psi$ *iff for all $d \in D$ we have $D, T, \mathcal{C}_\Pi, \mathcal{C}[x \mapsto d], n \vDash \psi;$*
- $\neg, \vee, \mathbf{X}, \mathbf{U}$ *connectives follows the inductive definition of LTL semantics.*
- $\mathbf{F}$ *and $\mathbf{G}$ connectives are defined and used as in LTL.*

We can now formally define what it means for a specification to satisfy an HyperFOLTL property.

---

[1] r_π denotes the relation r interpreted within the trace π. In order to simplify Hyper-FOLTL formulas, we sometimes write r_i to denotes r_{π_i}.

Definition 6 (Satisfaction). *Let* **Spec** *be an FO transition system and ϕ an HyperFOLTL formula, then we say that* **Spec** $\models \phi$ *if, for any domain D and for T, the set of traces of* **Spec** *with domain D, we have: $D, T, [], [], 0 \models \phi$.*

Remark 1 (Encoding of HyperFOLTL Satisfaction). The problem of checking if an FO transition system satisfy a HyperFOLTL formula can be reduced to the problem of satisfiability of an FOLTL formula [12]. However, the obtained FOLTL formula does not describe an FO transition system. Consequently, invariant-based methods are insufficient for proving unsatisfiability.

4   Application to the Leader Election Protocol

We'll now apply this formalism to our example, the leader election protocol.

4.1   Formal Specification of the Leader Election Protocol

Now, we can define the formal specification of the leader election protocol as an FO transition system (Σ, ι, τ). The signature Σ defines the components of the protocol, represented as sorts, relations and function symbols:

- Node is the sort of all nodes in the ring and Id is the sort of identifiers;
- id : Node $\rightarrow$ Id is the function associating each node with its identifier;
- **succ** : Node $\times$ Node is the relation indicating that two nodes are successors in the ring;
- **msgs** : Node $\times$ Id is the relation indicating that a node has an identifier in its message list.

Then, ι is the formula specifying the initial states of the protocol and consists in two parts. First, we define general axioms denoted by the formula **Ring**, which specify that the system comprises a ring-shaped network whose nodes have unique identifiers, describing a ring-shaped network by using a ternary relation [23].

$$\mathbf{Ring} := \forall x, y \cdot (x \neq y \Rightarrow \mathrm{id}(x) \neq \mathrm{id}(y)) \wedge \mathbf{Topology}$$
$$\mathbf{Topology} := \forall x, y, z \cdot \mathrm{btw}(x, y, z) \Rightarrow \mathrm{btw}(y, z, x)$$
$$\wedge \forall w, x, y, z \cdot \mathrm{btw}(w, x, y) \wedge \mathrm{btw}(w, y, z) \Rightarrow \mathrm{btw}(w, x, z)$$
$$\wedge \forall w, x, y \cdot \mathrm{btw}(w, x, y) \Rightarrow \neg\mathrm{btw}(w, y, x)$$
$$\wedge \forall w, x, y \cdot (w \neq x \wedge w \neq y \wedge x \neq y) \Rightarrow \mathrm{btw}(w, x, y) \vee \mathrm{btw}(w, y, x)$$
$$\wedge \forall x, y \cdot \mathbf{succ}(x, y) \Leftrightarrow (\forall z \cdot (z \neq x \wedge z \neq y) \Rightarrow \mathrm{btw}(x, y, z))$$

Then, we specify the rest of the initial states, i.e., that any **msgs** node list contains only the node's own identifier.

$$\mathbf{Init} := \forall x : \mathrm{Node}, i : \mathrm{Id} \cdot \mathbf{msgs}(x, i) \Leftrightarrow i = \mathrm{id}(x) \wedge \mathbf{Ring}$$

Finally, τ is the transition formula for the leader election protocol. In this protocol, the only possible operation is a node sending an identifier contained in its

msgs list to its successor. The successor adds this identifier to its own **msgs** list if it is greater than or equal to its own identifier. Additionally, we need to specify what does not change using two formulas, unchanged$_{\mathbf{msgs}}(s, r : \text{Node}, m : \text{Id})$ and unchanged$_{\mathbf{succ}}$, referred to as frame conditions:

$$\text{unchanged}_{\mathbf{msgs}}(s, r : \text{Node}, m : \text{Id}) := m < \text{id}(r) \Rightarrow (\mathbf{msgs}'(r, m) \Leftrightarrow \mathbf{msgs}(r, m))$$
$$\wedge \Big(\forall x : \text{Node}, i : \text{Id} \cdot (i \neq m \vee (x \neq s \wedge x \neq r)) \Rightarrow (\mathbf{msgs}(x, i) \Leftrightarrow \mathbf{msgs}'(x, i)) \Big)$$
$$\text{unchanged}_{\mathbf{succ}} := \forall x, y : \text{Node} \cdot \mathbf{succ}(x, y) \Leftrightarrow \mathbf{succ}'(x, y)$$

To simplify the specification of the desired hyperproperty, we introduce a formula: $\mathbf{SDef}(s) := \forall x : \text{Node} \cdot (\mathbf{Send}(x) \Leftrightarrow x = s)$ and a relation **Send** to label nodes performing the sending operation. Thus, the transition formula is:

$$\mathbf{Trans} := \exists s, r : \text{Node}, m : \text{id} \cdot \mathbf{SDef}(s) \wedge \mathbf{succ}(s, r) \wedge (m \geq \text{id}(r) \Rightarrow \mathbf{msgs}'(r, m))$$
$$\wedge \mathbf{msgs}(s, m) \wedge \neg \mathbf{msgs}'(s, m) \wedge \text{unchanged}_{\mathbf{msgs}}(s, r, m) \wedge \text{unchanged}_{\mathbf{succ}}$$

Our goal, in the context of the leader election protocol, is to determine whether an attacker can infer node identifiers based on observed message exchanges. Formally, we aim to verify that, for every possible identifier distribution and message-sending sequence, a trace exists that is consistent with both, which can be expressed as the following HyperFOLTL formula[2]:

$$\forall \pi_1, \pi_2 \cdot \exists \pi_3 \cdot (\forall n : \text{Node} \cdot \text{id}_2(n) = \text{id}_3(n)) \wedge$$
$$\mathbf{G}(\forall n : \text{Node} \cdot \mathbf{Send}_1(n) \Leftrightarrow \mathbf{Send}_3(n))$$

This property asserts that for any two traces of the protocol, there exists a third trace that aligns with the first trace in terms of the order of sent operations and with the second trace in terms of identifiers. This characteristic falls under the category of non-interference properties, signifying that the identifiers distribution has no consequence on determining which node sends a message.

4.2 Detecting a Violation of the Property

The leader election protocol, as specified in the previous section, violates the intended non-interference policy. This occurs because a node discards messages if the received identifier is lower than its own. To grasp the issue, consider a two-node ring where the following sequence of messages is exchanged: Node 1 sends to Node 2; Node 2 sends to Node 1; Node 2 sends to Node 1. In this scenario, it can be deduced that at least one of the two messages sent by Node 2 contains the identifier of Node 1. Consequently, Node 1's identifier is greater than Node 2's, leading to Node 1 being elected as the leader by the end of the sequence.

Now that we have identified the violation of this property, our focus shifts to detecting such violations in a general context. As observed, the property is infringed even in a network comprising only two nodes. Additionally, the

---

[2] we recall that in such a formula, r_i is used to represent the relation r interpreted in the trace π_i.

model-checking process of HyperFOLTL on a bounded domain can be simplified by transforming it into the model-checking of HyperLTL. This transformation involves unfolding the first-order quantifiers within the specified bounded domain. Since non-interference properties for finite-state systems fall within the decidable **HyperLTL$_2$** fragment of HyperLTL [5], we can effectively assess violations of this property within the given bounded domain. For the leader election protocol, this domain comprises only 2 nodes. This method effectively identifies counter-examples, but there is no general way to compute a completeness threshold. In other words, the absence of a counter-example does not rule out its existence in a larger scope. For instance, in the leader election protocol, if no counter-examples are found with fewer than 3 nodes, they may still exist with 4 or more nodes.

4.3 Proving the Satisfaction of the Property

Having identified a violation of the non-interference policy within the leader election protocol, a straightforward correction can be proposed to align with the non-interference policy. This correction is simple: allowing any node to send a message containing its own identifier at any given time. With this adjustment, all nodes can transmit messages continuously, ensuring that no discernible information can be deduced from these transmissions. Thus, the new transition formula is:

$$\textbf{Trans} := \exists s, r : \text{Node}, m : \text{id} \cdot (\textbf{Sending}(s, r, m) \vee \textbf{OwnSending}(s, r, m))$$
$$\wedge \, \text{unchanged}_{\textbf{msgs}}(s, r, m) \wedge \text{unchanged}_{\text{succ}}$$

where $\textbf{Sending}(s, r, m)$ corresponds to the initial sending operation and $\textbf{OwnSending}(s, r, m)$ corresponds to the sending of its own identifier:

$$\textbf{Sending}(s, r, m) := \textbf{SDef}(s) \wedge \text{succ}(s, r) \wedge \textbf{msgs}(s, m)$$
$$\wedge \, \neg\textbf{msgs}'(s, m) \wedge (m \geq \text{id}(r) \Rightarrow \textbf{msgs}'(r, m))$$
$$\textbf{OwnSending}(s, r, m) := \textbf{SDef}(s) \wedge \text{succ}(s, r) \wedge m = \text{id}(s)$$
$$\wedge \, (\textbf{msgs}(s, m) \Leftrightarrow \textbf{msgs}'(s, m)) \wedge (m \geq \text{id}(r) \Rightarrow \textbf{msgs}'(r, m))$$

Remark 2. For trace properties, correcting a protocol or a system is done by preventing some error traces to occur. However, the previous modification corrects the leader election protocol by enlarging the set of possible trace, demonstrating that non-interference is not a trace property.

While it might be apparent that the property is now satisfied, a question arises: how can this be rigorously proven in this context? The proof can be established through the utilization of a novel method relying on an FO formula that we call *linking invariant* which establishes relationships between the states and transitions of multiple traces in a system. Section 5 provides a formal definition of the concept of a linking invariant.

In the following, we will illustrate the application of this concept to three traces to satisfy the HyperFOLTL formula in the context of the leader election protocol. A linking invariant is used to construct states of the third trace π_3 from the states of π_1 and π_2. This linking invariant is presented as a first-order formula on relations describing the states of all three traces. In the case of the modified leader election, the linking invariant is the following:

$$L := \forall n : \text{Node} \cdot \text{id}_2(n) = \text{id}_3(n) \wedge (\textbf{Send}_1(n) \Leftrightarrow \textbf{Send}_3(n))$$
$$\wedge \forall n_1, n_2 : \text{Node} \cdot (\text{succ}_1(n_1, n_2) \Leftrightarrow \text{succ}_2(n_1, n_2) \Leftrightarrow \text{succ}_3(n_1, n_2))$$

In the following, Σ_1, Σ_2, and Σ_3 represent the symbols' signatures for respectively the first, second, and third traces referred by the HyperFOLTL formula. To proceed, the linking invariant L must satisfy the following conditions: (1) There exists an initial linking condition, L_i, s. t. $L_i \vDash L$ and for any possible valuation of the signature corresponding to universally quantified traces, there exists a valuation of the remaining relation that satisfies the formula; In simpler terms, the initial condition L_i must be robust enough to guarantee L under all possible initial settings for the system's traces. (2) $L_i \vDash \phi$ where ϕ is the FO formula obtained after removing the path quantifiers and the **G** operator; (3) For any couple of models $(\mathcal{M}, \mathcal{M}')$ satisfying L and the transition formula, there is a model $\mathcal{M}_L$ of L with same valuation than $\mathcal{M}'$ outside of Σ_3. This ensures that the linking invariant L can be maintained consistently across different system states and transitions, with $\mathcal{M}_L$ aligning with $\mathcal{M}'$ for all variables not in Σ_3.

The challenge lies in verifying the previous conditions. Condition (1) ensures that for any initial state corresponding to universally quantified traces, we can find initial states for the existentially quantified traces such that the Linking Invariant is satisfied at the start. In the leader election protocol, the initial linking condition states that we copy the initial state of trace 2 except for the **Send** relation that is taken from trace 1. Since the relation copied from trace 1 and trace 2 are distinct, the satisfaction of condition (1) is trivial. Then, condition (2) constitutes a standard first-order logic problem, solvable through a decidable fragment of FO or a sound reasoning method. Condition (3) ensures that from any combination of states satisfying the linking invariant, whatever the universally quantified traces do, there is a way to satisfy the Linking Invariant by choosing well the next states for existentially quantified traces. By induction, conditions (1) and (3) allow to prove the HyperFOLTL formula: $Q_1 \, pi_1, ..., Q_n \, pi_n$. $\text{G}(L)$. Our proposed approach for verifying condition (3) assumes that any transition is limited to modifying the values of relations within a bounded set of elements in the domain, denoted as $y_1 \ldots y_k$. This requirement is typically satisfied by distributed systems [22]. Given this assumption, verifying this condition can be simplified to a Quantified Boolean Formula (QBF) problem by examining the unfolding of the formula on the elements $y_1 \ldots y_k$ that undergo modification. For the leader election protocol, the modified relations are **Send** on s and **msgs** on (s, i) and (r, i). If, for any potential modification to these values for π_1 and π_2, it remains feasible to define values for π_3 while maintaining the linking invariant, it can be deduced that condition (3) is met. Let us define that $\textbf{Sending}_i$ (or $\textbf{OwnSending}_i$) represents **Sending** (or **OwnSending**) with all instances of any relation symbol r replaced by r_i, and **InvPreservation**(s, r) represents the fact that the linking invariant is satisfied on s and r before and after a transition. Hence, our proposed method gives the following formula:

$$\Big((\textbf{Sending}_1(s, r, m) \vee \textbf{OwnSending}_1(s, r, m))$$

$$\wedge \big(\textbf{Sending}_2(s, r, m) \vee \textbf{OwnSending}_2(s, r, m)\big)\Big)$$

$$\Rightarrow \Big((\textbf{Sending}_3(s, r, m) \vee \textbf{OwnSending}_3(s, r, m)) \wedge \textbf{InvPreservation}(s, r)\Big)$$

$$\textbf{InvPreservation}(s, r) := \Big(\big(\bigwedge_{n \in \{s,r\}} \text{id}_2(n) = \text{id}_3(n) \wedge (\textbf{Send}_1(n) \Leftrightarrow \textbf{Send}_3(n))\big)$$

$$\wedge \big(\bigwedge_{n_1, n_2 \in \{s,r\}} (\text{succ}_1(n_1, n_2) \Leftrightarrow \text{succ}_2(n_1, n_2) \Leftrightarrow \text{succ}_3(n_1, n_2))\big)\Big)$$

$$\Rightarrow \Big(\big(\bigwedge_{n \in \{s,r\}} \text{id}'_2(n) = \text{id}'_3(n) \wedge (\textbf{Send}'_1(n) \Leftrightarrow \textbf{Send}'_3(n))\big)$$

$$\wedge \big(\bigwedge_{n_1, n_2 \in \{s,r\}} (\text{succ}'_1(n_1, n_2) \Leftrightarrow \text{succ}'_2(n_1, n_2) \Leftrightarrow \text{succ}'_3(n_1, n_2))\big)\Big)$$

To confirm condition (3) for the leader election protocol, one can solve the QBF problem using the preceding formula. This involves universal quantification of relations associated to traces π_1 and π_2, and for relations on trace π_3, existential quantification if primed and universal quantification otherwise.

5   Formalizing Linking Invariant

This section provides a formal definition of the linking invariant concept and presents a sketch of a proof for proving condition 3 to satisfy this latter.

Definition 7 (Linking invariant). *Let L and P be FO formulas on Σ^{*3} and $TS = (\Sigma, \iota, \tau)$ be an FO transition system, L is said to be a linking invariant proving $\forall \pi_1, \dots \pi_n, \exists \pi_{n+1}, \dots \pi_m \mathbf{G}(P)$ for TS if:*

- *There exists L_i an FO formula on Σ^* such that:*
  - *for any structures $s_1, s_2, \dots, s_n$ satisfying ι, there is $s_{n+1}, \dots, s_m$ satisfying ι such that $s_1, s_2, \dots, s_m \vDash L_i$[4];*
  - *$L_i \vDash L$;*
- *$L \vDash P$.*
- *For all $s_1, s_2, \dots, s_m, s'_1, \dots, s'_n$ s.t. $s_1, \dots, s_m \vDash L$ and $\forall 1 \le i \le n, s_i, s'_i \vDash \tau$, there id $s'_{n+1}, \dots, s'_m$ s.t. $s'_1, \dots, s'_m \vDash L$ and $\forall n+1 \le i \le m, s_i, s'_i \vDash \tau$.*

---

[3] Σ^* represents the signature obtained by duplicating relations in Σ for all trace quantifiers appearing in the HyperFOLTL formula we are trying to prove.

[4] The notation $s_1, s_2, \dots, s_m \vDash L_i$ is used to compose the FO structures for evaluating the formula so s_1 is used for symbols from Σ_1, s_2 for Σ_2, etc.

The above definition states that (1) an initial condition ensuring L holds at the start, (2) L guarantees the desired property P, and (3) L is preserved across transitions. Then, the following result can be proved from a simple induction.

Theorem 1 (Linking invariant). *If* TS *admits a linking invariant proving* $\forall \pi_1, \ldots \pi_n, \exists \pi_{n+1}, \ldots \pi_m \mathbf{G}(P)$ *then:* TS $\models \forall \pi_1, \ldots \pi_k, \exists \pi_{k+1}, \ldots \pi_n \mathbf{G}(P)$

Theorem 2 (Criteria for condition 3). *Let's assume that τ restricts changes of values to a finite set of terms[5] and that L is a universally quantified formula, then checking condition (3) can be reduced to a QBF problem.*

Proof. First, we define some notations. Let ϕ be an FO formula, then ϕ_i is the formula where all relation r of ϕ are replaced by r_i, denoting the relation r interpreted in the i-th trace. Analogously, ϕ' denotes ϕ where all its relation symbols r are replaced by r' representing the value of r at the next instant in time. Then, we say that $m_1, \ldots, m_i, m_1', \ldots m_j' \models \phi$ if ϕ is true when interpreting all relation of the form r_k (resp. r_k') in structure m_k (resp. m_k'). Then we say that $m_1, \ldots, m_i, m_1', \ldots m_j'$ satisfy ϕ.

Finally, if E is a set of boolean variables, $Q_B E (Q \in \{\forall, \exists\})$ denotes the boolean quantifiers applied on all variables in E.

Let $m_1, \ldots, m_n, m_1', \ldots, m_k'$ be a list of structures such that there is no structures $m_{k+1}', \ldots m_n'$ satisfying $L \wedge \tau_1 \wedge \ldots \wedge \tau_m \wedge L'$. So either :

1. $L \wedge \tau_1 \wedge \ldots \tau_k$ is not satisfied by $m_1, \ldots, m_n, m_1', \ldots, m_k'$;
2. for any $m_{k+1}', \ldots m_n'$, $m_1, \ldots, m_n, m_1', \ldots, m_n'$ do not satisfy $\tau_{k+1} \wedge \ldots \tau_n \wedge L'$.

If condition 1 is verified then we are considering structures that either does not satisfy the linking invariant or structures that are not valid successor considering our FO transition system. So, we can assume that condition 2 is verified.

We define $Y_i' = \{r_i'(\boldsymbol{y}) \in \mathcal{R} \mid \boldsymbol{y} \in \{y_1, \ldots y_n\}^\star\}$, $Y' = \bigcup_{i > k} Y_i'$ and A the set of atoms (relation applied to terms) in $L \wedge \tau_1 \wedge \ldots \wedge \tau_m \wedge L'$.

ϕ^B the boolean formula obtained by removing all FO quantifiers from ϕ. ϕ_D is the boolean formula obtained by unfolding all FO quantifiers on a finite domain D. In the following, D will denotes all constants and variables appearing in L and τ. If condition 2 is not satisfied, we have a counterexample to the QBF problem[6]: $P_{QBF} = \forall_B A \setminus Y' \exists_B Y' \cdot L^B \wedge (\bigwedge_{1 \leq i \leq k} \tau_i^B) \Rightarrow (\bigwedge_{k+1 \leq j \leq n} \tau_j^B) \wedge L_D'$

Indeed, values for universally quantified variables can be taken from the structures $m_1, \ldots, m_n, m_1', \ldots, m_k'$. Then, if the QBF problem could be solved by completing the remaining boolean variables, then we would be able to define the new values of the finite set of relations whose values change during the transition. Moreover, L_D' is verified and because it unfolds the universal quantifiers of L' on

---

[5] τ is of the form $\exists y_1, \ldots, y_n \cdot \forall x_1, \ldots, x_m \cdot x_1, \ldots, x_m \notin F \Rightarrow NoChange(x_1, \ldots, x_m) \wedge \Phi_F(y_1, \ldots, y_n)$. Where $NoChange$ means that all relation on these variables keeps the same value after the transition.

[6] This construction can be improved to simplify the resulting QBF problem, but the proof of correctness becomes harder.

all combination for which values of relations have changed we can conclude that those new values satisfy L'. Then, it is possible to define $m'_{k+1}, \ldots m'_n$ such that $m_1, \ldots, m_n, m'_1, \ldots, m'_n$ satisfy $\tau_{k+1} \wedge \ldots \tau_n \wedge L'$, contradicting our hypothesis. We conclude that if P_{QBF} is true, condition (3) is satisfied.

6 Related Work

Formal verification of security policy is an active area of research. Some works, such as [26], introduce type systems to ensure secure information flow in programming languages and systems. However, they face challenges in considering all possible executions, leading to undecidable problems and the need for approximations, reducing accuracy. Other works, like [15], focus on non-interference enforcement in real-time systems using timed automata, verify non-interference property based on different behavior notions: trace equivalence, reachability equivalence, etc. However, it is limited to finite-state systems. Approaches discussed in [1] and [14] also employ methodologies based on timed automata along with timed non-interference to capture interference-free systems, particularly those with high-frequency actions. Infinite-state system verification, as discussed in [3], relies on finite-state abstraction, with no guarantee of finding suitable abstractions. Specific methods, as outlined in [12], address security policy verification in multi-agent workflows, a specific subset of distributed systems, by encoding HyperFOLTL formulas into decidable fragments of FOLTL, for which satisfiability can be reduced to finite-state model-checking. Nevertheless, strict system requirements must be met to ensure that the problem encoding falls within a decidable fragment of FOLTL. Another approach, presented in [21], reduces the problem of verifying security policies in multi-agent workflows to the inference and verification of an inductive invariant but also demands strict system requirements. Meanwhile, methods introduced in [11] focus on addressing hyperproperties in infinite-state systems without relying on finite-state abstraction, primarily by disproving hyperproperties by identifying counter-examples rather than formally proving their satisfaction. Other works, such as [9] and [8], focuses on deductive verification using generalized version of Hoare logic for proving hyperproperties on programs. The notion of linking invariant generalizes some ideas used in those proof techniques to distributed systems.

7 Conclusion

In this paper, we demonstrate the applicability of FO transition systems and HyperFOLTL formulas to express non-interference policies in distributed systems, using the leader election protocol as an example. We explore a potential approach for formally verifying such properties. Future work will involve formalizing the conditions proposed in Sect. 4.3 as a general deduction rule, implementing the automatic verification of the proposed methodology and evaluating its effectiveness. We also intend to extend our approach to cover other hyperproperties.

References

1. Barbuti, R., Tesei, L.: A decidable notion of timed non-interference. Fund. Inform. **54**(2–3), 137–150 (2003)
2. Bell, D., Padula, L.: Secure Computer Systems: Mathematical Foundations and Model. Mitre Corporation (1973). https://books.google.fr/books?id=y_SNPAAACAAJ
3. Beutner, R., Finkbeiner, B.: Software verification of hyperproperties beyond k-safety. In: Shoham, S., Vizel, Y. (eds.) Computer Aided Verification, pp. 341–362. Springer, Cham (2022)
4. Chang, E., Roberts, R.: An improved algorithm for decentralized extrema-finding in circular configurations of processes. Commun. ACM **22**(5), 281–283 (1979). https://doi.org/10.1145/359104.359108
5. Clarkson, M.R., Finkbeiner, B., Koleini, M., Micinski, K.K., Rabe, M.N., Sánchez, C.: Temporal logics for hyperproperties. CoRR **abs/1401.4492** (2014). http://arxiv.org/abs/1401.4492
6. Clarkson, M.R., Schneider, F.B.: Hyperproperties. In: 2008 21st IEEE Computer Security Foundations Symposium, pp. 51–65 (2008). https://doi.org/10.1109/CSF.2008.7
7. Conchon, S., Goel, A., Krstic, S., Mebsout, A., Zaïdi, F.: Cubicle: a parallel smt-based model checker for parameterized systems - tool paper. In: CAV, pp. 718–724 (2012)
8. Dardinier, T., Müller, P.: Hyper hoare logic: (dis-)proving program hyperproperties. In: Proceedings of the ACM on Programming Languages, vol. 8, pp. 1485–1509 (2024). https://doi.org/10.1145/3656437
9. Dickerson, R., Ye, Q., Zhang, M.K., Delaware, B.: RHLE: modular deductive verification of relational ∀∃ properties. In: Programming Languages and Systems: 20th Asian Symposium, APLAS 2022, Auckland, New Zealand, December 5, 2022, Proceedings, pp. 67–87. Springer, Heidelberg (2022). https://doi.org/10.1007/978-3-031-21037-2_4
10. Finkbeiner, B.: Temporal hyperproperties. Bull. EATCS **123** (2017)
11. Finkbeiner, B., Frenkel, H., Hofmann, J., Lohse, J.: Automata-based software model checking of hyperproperties (2023)
12. Finkbeiner, B., Müller, C., Seidl, H., Zălinescu, E.: Verifying security policies in multi-agent workflows with loops. In: Proceedings of the 2017 ACM SIGSAC Conference on Computer and Communications Security. pp. 633–645. CCS 2017. Association for Computing Machinery, New York (2017). https://doi.org/10.1145/3133956.3134080
13. Finkbeiner, B., Zimmermann, M.: The first-order logic of hyperproperties. CoRR **abs/1610.04388** (2016). http://arxiv.org/abs/1610.04388
14. Focardi, R., Gorrieri, R., Martinelli, F.: Real-time information flow analysis. IEEE J. Sel. Areas Commun. **21**(1), 20–35 (2003). https://doi.org/10.1109/JSAC.2002.806122
15. Gardey, G., Mullins, J., Roux, O.H.: Non-interference control synthesis for security timed automata. Electronic Notes in Theoretical Computer Science **180**(1), 35–53 (2007). https://doi.org/10.1016/j.entcs.2005.05.046, https://www.sciencedirect.com/science/article/pii/S1571066107003143, proceedings of the International Workshop on Security and Concurrency (SecCo 2005)
16. Ghosal, S., Shyamasundar, R.K.: A generalized notion of non-interference for flow security of sequential and concurrent programs. In: 2020 27th Asia-Pacific

Software Engineering Conference (APSEC), pp. 51–60 (2020). https://doi.org/10.1109/APSEC51365.2020.00013

17. Goguen, J.A., Meseguer, J.: Security policies and security models. In: 1982 IEEE Symposium on Security and Privacy, pp. 11–20 (1982). https://doi.org/10.1109/SP.1982.10014

18. Lamport, L.: A simple approach to specifying concurrent systems. Commun. ACM **32**(1), 32-45 (1989). https://doi.org/10.1145/63238.63240

19. Lamport, L.: Specifying Systems: The TLA+ Language and Tools for Hardware and Software Engineers. Addison-Wesley Longman Publishing Co., Inc, USA (2002)

20. Macedo, N., Brunel, J., Chemouil, D., Cunha, A., Kuperberg, D.: Lightweight specification and analysis of dynamic systems with rich configurations. In: Proceedings of the 2016 24th ACM SIGSOFT International Symposium on Foundations of Software Engineering. pp. 373–383. FSE 2016. Association for Computing Machinery, New York (2016). https://doi.org/10.1145/2950290.2950318

21. Müller, C., Seidl, H., Zğlinescu, E.: Inductive invariants for noninterference in multi-agent workflows. In: 2018 IEEE 31st Computer Security Foundations Symposium (CSF), pp. 247–261 (2018). https://doi.org/10.1109/CSF.2018.00025

22. Padon, O., Hoenicke, J., Losa, G., Podelski, A., Sagiv, M., Shoham, S.: Reducing liveness to safety in first-order logic. Proc. ACM Program. Lang. **2**(POPL) (2017). https://doi.org/10.1145/3158114

23. Padon, O., McMillan, K.L., Panda, A., Sagiv, M., Shoham, S.: IVY: safety verification by interactive generalization. SIGPLAN Not. **51**(6), 614–630 (2016). https://doi.org/10.1145/2980983.2908118

24. Peyras, Q., Bodeveix, J.P., Brunel, J., Chemouil, D.: Sound verification procedures for temporal properties of infinite-state systems. In: Silva, A., Leino, K. (eds.) Computer Aided Verification, pp. 337–360. Springer, Cham (2021)

25. Pnueli, A.: The temporal logic of programs. In: 18th Annual Symposium on Foundations of Computer Science (SFCS 1977), pp. 46–57 (1977). https://doi.org/10.1109/SFCS.1977.32

26. Sabelfeld, A., Myers, A.: Language-based information-flow security. IEEE J. Sel. Areas Commun. **21**(1), 5–19 (2003). https://doi.org/10.1109/JSAC.2002.806121

27. Zimmermann, J., Mohay, G.: Distributed intrusion detection in clusters based on non-interference. In: Proceedings of the 2006 Australasian Workshops on Grid Computing and E-Research, vol. 54. pp. 89–95. ACSW Frontiers 2006, Australian Computer Society, Inc. (2006)

Deductive Verification of Sparse Sets in Why3

Catherine Dubois[(✉)]

ENSIIE, INRIA, Université Paris-Saclay, LMF, Gif-sur-Yvette, France
catherine.dubois@ensiie.fr

Abstract. To represent finite sets of integers on an interval 0..n, Briggs
and Torczon studied a very simple data structure in 1993, called *sparse
sets*. With this representation, initialization, membership test, insertion
and deletion of an element are O(1) operations. This data structure is
often used in compilers to allocate registers or to represent the objects
in a video game. A variant of this data structure is also used in finite
domain constraint solvers to represent the domains of integer variables.
This variant makes it a backtrackable data structure. We have formalized and verified the original data structure and its variant in Why3.
Set operations such as intersection and union are formally verified, even
though they are less commonly used with this representation of sets. To
our knowledge this is the first formal verification of the backtrackable
variant of sparse sets used as domains.

1 Introduction

Sets are seldom primitive objects in programming languages or specification formalisms. There are such objects in the old programming language Setl [18] or the
logic programming language {log} [8] and also in the formal languages B [1] or
Event-B [2] and TLA+ [12]. More usually, they are available as implementations
in libraries, based on underlying data structures such as sorted lists, red-black
trees, AVL trees, B trees, skiplists, etc. In this paper, we focus on sparse sets,
studied by Briggs and Torczon [4] in 1993, also appearing as an exercise in the
famous book "The Design and Analysis of Computer Algorithms" written by
Aho and Hopcroft [3]. This data structure dates back to computer folklore, it
is used in different applications like register allocation, video game, constraint
solving. With this mutable representation based on arrays and simple manipu-
lations, initialization, membership test, insertion and deletion of an element are
O(1) operations. Many implementations exist on the web, in several languages,
e.g. Java, C++, C, Rust.

Sparse sets appear as a benchmark (Constant-time sparse array) of VACID-0,
a suite of benchmark verification problems proposed in 2010 [15]. The sparse
sets data structure as described by Briggs and Torczon is a particular case of
the latter in which there is one less indirection. A solution[1] where 3 operations

---

[1] available at https://toccata.gitlabpages.inria.fr/toccata/gallery/vacid_0_sparse_
array.en.html.

J. Protzenko and A. Raad (Eds.): VSTTE 2024, LNCS 15525, pp. 28–46, 2025.
https://doi.org/10.1007/978-3-031-86695-1_3

(membership, add and remove) are implemented, has been given using Why3 by Filliâtre and Paskevich.

Sparse sets are also used in constraint solvers as an alternative to range sequences or bit vectors for implementing domains of integer variables [13] which are nothing else than mathematical finite sets of integers. Sparse sets as domains are slightly different from sparse sets introduced by Briggs and Torczon making them very easy to store and restore when backtracking for finding solutions.

Our main contribution is a formally verified implementation of sparse sets as domains and its various operations, developed with the deductive verification tool Why3 [10], extracted in OCaml. In addition to classical set operations (test membership, remove, etc.), we specify and verify an operation that allows the user to undo some operations very easily (in one simple assignment). This contribution brings some more confidence in the data structures used in constraint solvers, as it has been done by Ledein and Dubois [14] for the traditional implementation of domains as range sequences.

In [7], Cristiá and the author have formalized this sparse set as domain variant and verified three simple operations (remove, bind and membership) in three formalisms, Why3, EventB and {log}. However they do not address the verification of the backtrackable dimension and in particular the undo operation.

The article is structured as follows. In Sect. 2 we give an informal overview of sparse sets. In Sect. 3, we briefly introduce Why3 and WhyML. In Sect. 4, we detail our WhyML implementation of sparse sets following Briggs and Torczon and discuss its deductive verification. In Sect. 5, we introduce the modifications to the previous data structure when it is used to represent the domain of integer variables in constraint solvers. Then, in Sect. 6, we present the WhyML formalization of this backtrackable variant by focusing mainly on the additional artefacts we used to verify the undo operation. Section 7 presents some experimentations performed on the OCaml code extracted from our models. Finally we conclude and present some future work.

All the code described in this paper is available on https://gitlab.com/ cdubois/why3_sparsesets.

2   Sparse Sets

Sparse sets are used to represent subsets of natural numbers up to $N-1$, where N is any non-zero natural number. The range $[0..N-1]$ is called the universe of the sparse set in the following. A sparse set D is represented by two arrays of length N called $Dense$ and $Sparse$, and a natural number $sizeD$[2]. The current elements of the finite set are those in $Dense[0, sizeD - 1]$—let us call this subarray the effective part —, the rest of the array being $garbage$. The array $Sparse$ maps any value $v \in [0, N-1]$ to an index ind_v in $Dense$ or is not initialized. Thus, for the current elements v of the set, $Sparse[v]$ has a value i in the range $[0, sizeD - 1]$

---

[2] The name of this data structure may be explained by the fact that the $Sparse$ array may have holes whereas the $Dense$ array is more compact.

and *Dense*[i] is equal to v. If D is empty (resp. the full set), *sizeD* is equal to 0 (resp. N).

The two invariants of the data structure representing the set D are as follows:

$$D \subseteq 0..N - 1 \wedge D = \{Dense[i] \mid 0 \le i < sizeD\} \qquad (P_1)$$
$$v \in D \iff 0 \le Sparse[v] < sizeD \wedge Dense[Sparse[v]] = v \qquad (P_2)$$

Figure 1a illustrates this representation. This state has been reached after inserting the elements 3, 6, 4, 7, 5 and 8 in the empty set. The blue arrows emphasize the invariant P_2.

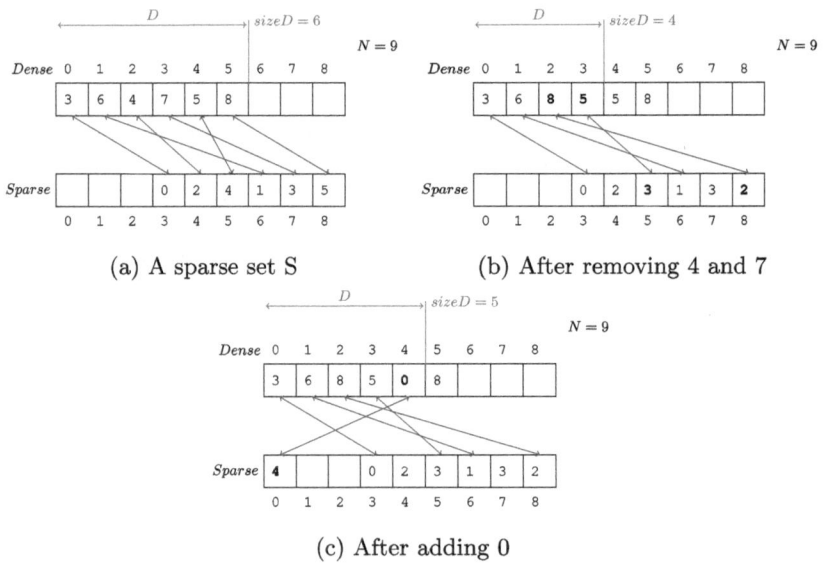

(a) A sparse set S   (b) After removing 4 and 7

(c) After adding 0

Fig. 1. Three States of a Sparse Set

Checking if an element v belongs to the sparse set D simply consists in the evaluation of the expression $0 \le Sparse[v] < sizeD$ && $Dense[Sparse[v]] = v$. Removing an element consists in replacing v in *Dense* with the last element e of the *Dense* effective part ($e = Dense[sizeD - 1]$), decrementing *sizeD* and updating *Sparse*[e]. This operation is illustrated in Fig. 1b: 4 and 7 are removed in this order from the sparse set represented in Fig. 1a. We can see two occurrences of both 8 and 5 but their presence in $Dense[sizeD..N]$ does not matter.

Inserting an element v is implemented as follows: put v in *Dense* at the position *sizeD*, update *Sparse*[v] with *sizeD* and increment *sizeD*. In Fig. 1c, 0 has been inserted in the sparse set represented in Fig. 1b.

Clearing the sparse set, that is making it represent the empty set, is very efficient, just set *sizeD* to 0. The cardinality of a sparse set is exactly the value of $sizeD$. All the previous operations are constant-time. Operations like forall, exists, union, intersection, equality only require to explore the elements in the effective part of $Dense$, and are thus in $O(sizeD)$.

3   Why3 and WhyML

Why3 [10] is a platform for deductive program verification that provides a specification and programming language called WhyML. It relies on external automated and interactive theorem provers to discharge automatically generated verification conditions (VC). The SMT provers Alt-ergo, CVC4 and Z3 are used here. Transformations, aka tactics, are also provided, making Why3 an interactive proof environment. Why3 supports modular verification and includes some mechanisms for managing modularity, abstraction and genericity [11].

WhyML allows the user to write functional or imperative programs featuring polymorphism, algebraic data types, pattern-matching, exceptions, mutable variables, arrays, etc. These programs can be specified by using contracts (pre- and post- conditions) and assertions (e.g. variants, loop invariants). User-defined types with invariants can be introduced, invariants are verified at the function call boundaries. Furthermore to prevent logical inconsistencies, Why3 generates a verification condition to ensure that such a type is inhabited. To help the verification, a witness can be explicitly given by the user (by clause in Fig. 3). The old operator can be used inside post-conditions to refer to the value of a term at the call program point.

In addition, as with other verification tools, ghost code can be used to annotate the source code in order to make it easier to verify. Ghost code is regular WhyML code, except that ghost variables or record fields are introduced using the keyword ghost.

Correct-by-construction OCaml (and, more recently, C) programs can be automatically extracted from verified WhyML programs. More detail is provided throughout the paper as necessary.

4   Formal Verification of Sparse Sets

This section deals with the data structure as it is described in Briggs and Torczon's paper [4]. We provide a WhyML specification and an implementation of the data structure and its operations.

4.1   Abstract Specification

We start with a high-level module that contains the abstract specification of type t and operations on that type, where t is the type of subsets of an interval of natural numbers (beginning at 0 as in [4]). Figure 2 contains an excerpt of that module. The type t here is specified as a record with two fields only used for specification: the size n of the support universe and setD which has to be

32   C. Dubois

understood as the high-level model of the data structure. The fset logical type constructor is defined in the module set.FsetInt of the standard library. Set mathematical symbols that appear in the contracts are used here and in the rest of the paper to denote the mathematical set operations acting on mathematical sets also defined in the module set.FsetInt. The == infix operator is the mathematical set equality. The writes clause in a contract indicates that the corresponding function updates its argument. The operations are implemented in the refining module that also provides a full definition for the type. We describe this refining module in the next subsection.

```
module FiniteNatSet
use int.Int
use set.FsetInt

type t  = abstract {n : int ;
                        mutable setD : fset int ; }
invariant {setD ⊆ (interval 0 n)}

val empty_set (nn : int) : t
requires {0<=nn}
ensures {result.setD = ∅}
ensures {result.n = nn}

val member (v : int) (a : t) : bool
requires {0<=v}
ensures {result = v ∈ a.setD}

val cardinal_sparse (a : t) : int
ensures {result = |a.setD|}

val add (v : int) (a : t) : unit
requires {0<=v<a.n}
ensures {a.setD ==   (old a.setD) ∪ {v} }
writes {a.setD}

val remove (v : int) (a : t) : unit
requires {0<=v<a.n}
ensures {a.setD == (old a.setD) − {v}}
writes {a.setD}

...

end
```

Fig. 2. Abstract Specification

4.2   Concrete Implementation

The abstract type t is implemented as the record type tsparse (see Fig. 3) whose fields are the size of the universe n, the two mutable arrays dense and sparse, the mutable bound sizeD and the ghost mathematical and abstract model setD. Why3 will generate verification conditions to ensure that the concrete implementation respects the abstract specification.

This record type definition is constrained by invariant properties: the length of both arrays is n which is a positive number, contents are belonging to the integer range 0..n − 1 (Inv1), sizeD is between 0 and n (Inv2), the two arrays must be consistent for those elements in the set (Inv3) (P_2 in Sect. 2). Furthermore the last property, Inv5, relates the abstract model with the concrete representation as in the property P_1 of Sect. 2.

In [4], Briggs and Torczon emphasize the fact that the two arrays do not require to be initialized when allocated. In the solution given by Filliâtre and Paskevich to the formal verification of sparse arrays, the arrays are not initialized too [9]. They specify a non initialized memory with the help of a malloc function. In our implementation we initialize the arrays dense and sparse with a negative value (−1) when they are created. We could have reused Filliâtre and Paskevich's approach in our formalization, but we did not in order to stay in line with the variant developed in the next section.

```
let constant initval : int = -1

predicate dom_ran (a : array int) (n: int) =
0 <= n && a.length = n && forall i. 0<=i<n -> initval<=a[i]< n

type tsparse =        { n : int;
                        mutable dense: array int;
                        mutable sparse: array int;
                        mutable sizeD: int;
                        mutable ghost setD : fset int; }
invariant {
   (*Inv1*)    dom_ran dense n && dom_ran sparse n &&
   (*Inv2*)    0 <= sizeD <= n &&
   (*Inv3*)    (forall i:int. 0 <= i < sizeD ->
                   (0 <= dense[i] && sparse[dense[i]] = i)) &&
   (*Inv4*)    setD ⊆ (interval 0 n) &&.
   (*Inv5*)    forall x: int. 0<= x < n -> (x ∈  setD <->
                   (0 <= sparse[x] < sizeD && dense[sparse[x]] = x))
}
by {n = 0; dense = make 0 initval; sparse = make 0 initval;
    sizeD = 0; setD = ∅}
```

Fig. 3. WhyML Type of a Sparse Set

The code of the operations on sparse sets are the straightforward translation of the algorithms in [4], except for the supplementary ghost code (e.g. the last statement in `remove_sparse`) which updates the abstract model `a.setD`. The deletion operation, named here `remove_sparse`, is shown in Fig. 4.

In addition to the previous constant-time operations, the following functions have been implemented and verified:

- forall: check if all the elements of the sparse set satisfy a predicate (linear with respect to the number of elements in `a.setD`);
- exists: check if one element of the sparse set satisfies a predicate (linear with respect to the number of elements in `a.setD`);
- tolist: compute the list of elements (linear with respect to the number of elements in `a.setD`);
- filter: remove the elements that do not satisfy a predicate (linear with respect to the number of elements in `a.setD`);
- copy: create a copy of a sparse set (linear wrt the number of elements in `a.setD`);
- union of 2 sparse sets: create a new sparse set containing the elements of the 2 arguments (linear wrt the number of elements in each set);
- in place union: update the first argument required to have the largest universe with the union of the 2 arguments (linear wrt the number of elements in the second argument);
- intersection of 2 sparse sets: create a new sparse set (linear wrt the number of the smallest set).
- in place intersection: update the first argument required to have the smallest universe with the intersection of the 2 arguments (linear wrt the number of elements in the first argument);

Let us notice that for the filter and in place intersection operations, iteration and removal are performed at the same time.

The deductive verification of all these operations required to invent and add some formal annotations such as loop invariants, ghost code and lemma functions. A typical example is the implementation of `cardinal_sparse` shown in Fig. 4. Its code is very simple since the number of elements in the sparse set a is exactly `a.sizeD` but a lemma-function, `cardinal_sizeD`, is used to prove the function's contract as a lemma that will be provided to the provers. The latter states that $|a.setD|$ = `a.sizeD` by going through the dense array up to `sizeD`, collecting and counting its elements. In all the operations or logical functions that require an iteration on the effective part of the Dense array, a ghost variable collects the visited elements (and also the elements removed, e.g. in the in place intersection operation) and allows the computation to be observed. This makes the WhyML code very verbose[3] but it is the prize to pay to have automatic proofs.

VCs for the functions concern the conformance of the code to the post-condition and also to the invariant attached to the tsparse type.

```
let remove_sparse (v : int) (a : tsparse)
requires {0<=v<a.n}
ensures {a.setD ==  (old a.setD) − {v}}
=
let i = a.sparse[v] in
if 0 <= i < a.sizeD && a.dense[i]=v then
  let e = a.dense[a.sizeD − 1] in
  a.dense[i] <- e ; a.sparse[e] <- i ;
  a.sizeD <- a.sizeD − 1;
  a.setD <- a.setD − {v}

(* a lemma function to help the verification *)
let lemma cardinal_sizeD  (a : tsparse)
ensures {|a.setD| = a.sizeD}
=
let ghost ref s = FsetInt.empty in
let ghost ref nb = 0 in
for i = 0 to a.sizeD − 1  do
  invariant {forall x:int. (exists j. 0<=j<i && x = a.dense[j]) <-> x ∈ s}
  invariant {nb = |s| && nb = i}
  s <- s ∪ {a.dense[i]};
  nb <- nb + 1
done ;
assert {a.setD == s && nb = a.sizeD }

let cardinal_sparse (a : tsparse) : int
ensures {result = |a.setD|}
=
return a.sizeD
```

Fig. 4. Implementation of Some Sparse Set Operations in WhyML

---

[3] 18 lines of logical code are added to the 8 lines of computational code in the in-place intersection operation.

4.3   Proofs

The proof of all the VCs are done automatically using three automatic provers, CVC4, Alt-Ergo and Z3, using the strategy Auto Level 2^4. Statistics per prover, number of proofs, time (minimum/maximum/average) in seconds, are recorded in Fig. 5.

Prover	nb.proofs	min.time(s)	max.time(s)	av.time(s)
Z3 4.8.9	1	0.06	0.06	0.06
Alt-Ergo 2.5.1	29	0.03	2.12	0.55
CVC4 1.6	276	0.03	1.80	0.15

Fig. 5. Sparse sets - Statistics per Prover: Number of Proofs, Time (minimum/maximum/average) in Seconds

4.4   Extraction of OCaml Executable Code

To extract OCaml executable code from this development, we modified the previous WhyML code to use machine integers instead of mathematical integers. However mathematical integers are still manipulated in most logical assertions or ghost code. In our case it requires only syntactical modifications regarding the type of integer variables and arrays and some insertions of coercions between machine integers and mathematical integers in the logical assertions. The proofs remain all automatic.

This data structure is also often proposed as a bounded data structure, in which the set is constrained to have at most a given cardinality m. We can find several implementations of this variant on the Web. In that case the length of the dense array is m. The abstract type t and the concrete type tsparse are modified to take into account this maximal capacity. Some functions (e.g. add and union) are also concerned with this limit. This new requirement does not bring any difficulty for the verification. We have implemented this variant in WhyML and verified it with Why3. When machine integers are used, the union function requires an additional pre-condition for not going to an overflow.

5   Backtrackable Sparse Sets as Domains

In this section we focus on a variant of sparse sets used in some constraint solvers (e.g. MiniCP [16], OsCaR [17]) to represent the domain of an integer variable, i.e. the finite set of possible values for that variable [13]. In such a context, to find a solution to a collection of constraints on some variables, or to show that the problem is unsatisfiable, the use case is as follows: for a variable X,

---

[4] and only one assertion in the lemma function about the cardinality.

initialize $Domain(X) = 0..N - 1$, for some N, then propagate constraints to prune $Domain(X)$, then set $Domain(X)$ to a singleton containing a value of the pruned domain, propagate again, etc., backtrack if necessary. Thus, once the domain is initialized, there is no need to add any value, only deletions are performed. The advantage of sparse sets, as we have seen, is that membership and deletion operations can be performed in constant time. Furthermore, with a simple variation, these data structures are easy to restore when exploring solutions in an imperative setting, making backtracking cheap. Even if they are not used in constraint solving, we keep in our verified implementation the add and union operations but we will have to take care of the fact that they break reversibility. In the rest of the paper, to refer to this variant, we sometimes use the expression *sparse sets as domains* or shortly *domains*.

In this variant, the property P_2 is enforced for every value in $Dense$ (not only in $Dense[0..sizeD - 1]$): $Sparse[Dense[i]] = i$ for all $i \in 0..N - 1$, called now P_2'. Checking the membership of value v becomes trivial: just check $Sparse[v] < sizeD$. Removing an element v now consists of swapping v with the last element in $Dense$, decrementing $sizeD$ and also updating $Sparse$. An example is shown in Fig. 6. As pointed out in [13], the values in $dense[sizeD..N-1]$ are not changed by any operation, in particular by a deletion as long as there are no insertions. Let us call this property P_3. This property can easily be added as an additional post-condition of the remove operation. The other operations remain the same (even if add and union are not used in constraint solving). We introduce a new function bind, which takes an argument v and reduces the set to the singleton $\{v\}$. It is useful in the context of constraint solving, to bind the value of a variable when exploring the search space. Its behaviour is very similar to remove: v is swapped with the last element in *sparse*, *dense* is updated accordingly, and $sizeD$ is set to 1. Illustrations are given in Fig. 6.

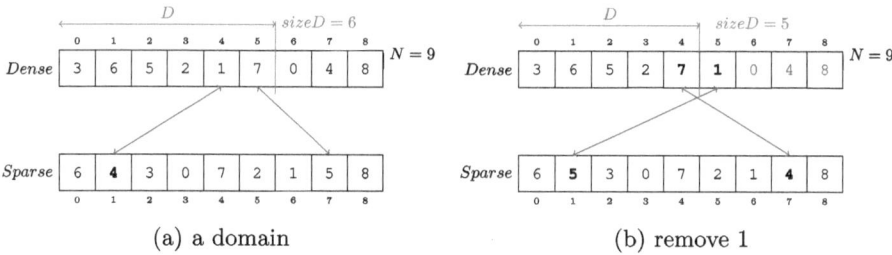

(a) a domain   (b) remove 1

Fig. 6. A sparse set as Domain and a Deletion

Sparse sets in this variant are now easily backtrackable (or reversible), the only element to be stored and restored being the value of $sizeD$. Figure 7 illustrates this with a simple example. Let a be the sparse set in Fig. 7a denoting the set D_0. We store the current value of $sizeD$, which is 6. Then we remove 1, 6 and 3 from a, whose resulting value is described on Fig. 7b. To restore the initial

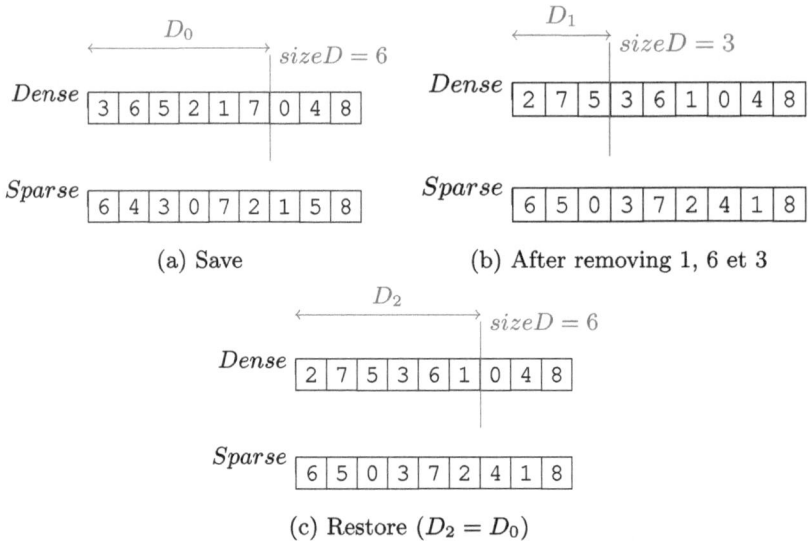

Fig. 7. Backtracking on a Sparse Set as Domain

situation, it is sufficient to set $sizeD$ to the value previously stored, i.e. 6, see Fig. 7c. We recover exactly the same mathematical set of elements, even if the values of the two arrays are different from the value in Fig. 7a. The behaviour is the same when backtracking after a `bind` operation, a `clear` operation or a destructive intersection operation, or a combination of all of these. However insertion and destructive union operations break this possibility, we keep them in our formalization but after their use, all checkpoint information is lost. We introduce the operation `undo` to come back to a previously reached situation, characterized by the value p of $sizeD$. Its algorithmic content is very simple, i.e. set $sizeD$ to p but its specification requires more work and it will affect all the operations since new invariants will be needed. The main idea is to keep, for a domain, the collection of all previous states to which we can go back.

6 Formal Verification of Sparse Sets as Domains

We follow the same approach with an abstract specification and a concrete implementation. To take into account P_2', we have to change the type invariant of the `tsparse` type. To specify `undo`, the modification is deeper and impacts both the abstract type `t` and the concrete type `tsparse`.

6.1 Abstract Specification

The type definition of the abstract type `t` is shown on Fig. 8. We introduce an additional abstract variable, `states`, of type `fmap (fset int)`, which stores the different successive states of the set, i.e. the successive mathematical models. It is defined as a partial function mapping cardinalities of setD to their corresponding model. For example, if n is 5, starting with the full set, removing 0 and then binding to the singleton containing 2, would result in the partial function states which maps 5 to the set $\{0,1,2,3,4\}$, 4 to $\{1,2,3,4\}$ and 1 to $\{2\}$ and which is defined nowhere else.

A theory of partial functions is available in the Why3 standard library. It specifies a partial function as a WhyML total function and a mathematical set corresponding to its definition domain. Several logical functions and predicates are provided. For example, the formula mapsto i s f expresses that i is in the definition domain of the partial function f and relates i with its image s.

Each time an operation that modifies the sparse set, is performed, its current mathematical model is stored in states: states (|setD|) is then defined and equal to setD. This is part of the invariant that needs to be preserved. As said before, backtracking is only possible if elements are only removed from the sparse set, this implies that states is defined from the maximum cardinality, i.e. n, to the current cardinality, and that the corresponding images are subsets of each other. Furthermore, because of the bind operation, we may step from a cardinality i to 1, which means that the domain of states may not be an interval. The predicate valid_states specifies the invariant properties expected of states. So the abstract type t is modified to take account of this additional invariant (in Fig. 8, modifications are marked with 2 stars).

Figure 8 also contains the abstract specification of the undo operation. It takes an argument that is the cardinality of the set to which to come back. This one must be greater than the cardinality of the current set and the corresponding state must have been encountered in the past, so its mathematical model must have been registered in states. The post-condition specifies that after calling the operation the current model is the one stored in states(p), and the previous states have not changed for cardinalities greater than p. The new value of states has to comply with the valid_states invariant property, so states is not defined anymore for cardinalities smaller than p after the undo operation. The abstract specification of other operations has to be adapted consequently (see remove and add in Fig. 8). The additional post-condition of add enforces that backtracking is no longer possible by restricting the definition domain of states to the singleton $\{|a.setD|\}$.

6.2   Concrete Implementation

The tsparse type is adapted in the same way as the abstract type t (see Fig. 9). An additional ghost variable states is introduced and constrained according to the valid_states property. Furthermore a new property, $Inv7$, makes the connection between states and sparse: if s is the mathematical set registered in states for i, then its elements are exactly those that are in dense$[0..i]$. Again as a property in the type invariant, it must be preserved by any operation modifying an argument of type tsparse. Furthermore $Inv3$ is modified to take into account that dense and sparse are now inverse and $Inv5$ is simplified.

```
predicate valid_states (states : fmap int (fset int) (setD : fset int) (n : int) =
-- domain of states is included in 0..n
   (dom states) ⊆ (interval |setD| (n+1)) &&
-- current state is registered
   mapsto |setD| setD states &&
-- each registered state contains the current one
   forall i:int, s : fset int. mapsto i s states ->
       s ⊆ (interval 0 n) && |setD| = i && setD ⊆ s

type t = abstract {n : int ; mutable setD : fset int ;
                   mutable states: fmap int (fset int);     (* *)
                   }
invariant {setD ⊆ (interval 0 n) &&
           valid_states states setD n}     (* *))

val remove (v : int) (a : t) : unit
requires {0<=v<a.n && v ∈ a.setD}
ensures {a.setD == remove v (old a.setD)}
ensures {forall i. 0 <= i <= a.n -> i ≠ |a.setD| ->
             (mapsto i x a.states <-> mapsto i x (old a).states)}     (* *)

val add (v : int) (a : t) : unit
requires {0<=v<a.n && v ∉ a.setD}
ensures {a.setD == add v (old a.setD)}
ensures {dom a.states = {|a.setD|}}     (* *))

val undo (a : t) (p : int) : unit
requires {|a.setD| < p <= a.n}
requires {p ∈ (dom states)}
writes {a.setD, a.states}
ensures {exists s. mapsto p s (old a).states && a.setD == s}
ensures {forall i. p < i <= a.n ->
             (mapsto i v a.states <-> mapsto i v (old a).states)}
```

Fig. 8. Abstract Type t and undo Abstract Specification

The code of the undo operation is shown in Fig. 9. Its contract is similar to that of the abstract specification. Its computational part is only the last statement, the rest is some ghost code to update the model (a.setD and a.states). In particular, to maintain the invariant, all states between a.sizeD and p are deleted in a.states, thanks to the remove_set_from_domain operation which removes from the definition domain of a partial function all the elements of its first argument. The operations for removing and inserting an element are also illustrated in that figure. The computational part is composed of the two first statements. Besides the modification of the a.setD ghost model, the ghost code updates the a.states partial function: the former operation just stores the current state while the latter also erases all the previous stored models.

6.3 Proofs

The proof of all the VCs are done automatically using three automatic provers, CVC4 and Alt-Ergo using the strategy Auto Level 2. Statistics per prover, number of proofs, time (minimum/maximum/average) in seconds, are recorded in Fig. 10.

```
type tsparse =      { n : int;
                      mutable dense: array int;
                      mutable sparse: array int;
                      mutable sizeD: int;
                      mutable ghost setD: fset int;
                      mutable ghost states: fmap (fset int);    (* *)
                    }
invariant {
(*Inv1 *)    dom_ran dense n && dom_ran sparse n &&
(*Inv2 *)    0 <= sizeD <= n &&
(*Inv3' *)   (forall i:int. 0 <= i <n && 0<=v<n->
                  (dense[i]=v <-> sparse[v]=i))
(*Inv4 *)    setD ⊆ (interval 0 n) &&.
(*Inv5' *)   (forall x: int. 0<= x < n ->
                  (x ∈  setD <-> sparse[x] < sizeD)) &&
(*Inv6 *)    valid_states states setD n &&.    (* *)
(*Inv7 *)    (forall i, s. 0<=i<=n -> states i =  s ->
                  (forall x. 0<=x<n  -> (sparse[x]<i <-> mem x s)))    (* *)
}
by ...

let undo_sparse (a : tsparse) (p : int) : unit
...
=
let ghost v = fmap_apply a.states p in
 a.setD <-  v ;
 a.states <- remove_set_from_domain (interval 0 p) a.states;
 a.sizeD <- p

let remove_sparse (v : int) (a : tsparse)
...
=
swap_two_arrays a.dense a.sparse a.n a.sparse[v] (a.sizeD - 1);
a.sizeD <- a.sizeD - 1;
a.setD <- remove v a.setD;
a.states <- fmap_add a.sizeD a.setD a.states    (* *)

let add_sparse (v : int) (a : tsparse)
...
=
swap_two_arrays a.dense a.sparse a.n a.sparse[v] a.sizeD;
a.sizeD <- a.sizeD + 1;
a.setD <- add v a.setD;
a.states <- fmap_add a.sizeD a.setD fmap_empty    (* *)
```

Fig. 9. Concrete Implementation of Domains

6.4 Extraction of OCaml Executable Code

OCaml executable code has been extracted. Again the previous implementation of sparse sets as domains has been modified to deal with machine integers without any difficulty. Proofs are still automatic.

Prover	nb.proofs	min.time(s)	max.time(s)	av.time(s)
Z3 4.8.9	39	0.02	0.96	0.08
Alt-Ergo 2.5.1	115	0.01	3.74	0.22
CVC4 1.6	216	0.04	1.07	0.15

Fig. 10. Statistics per prover: number of proofs, time (minimum/maximum/average) in seconds

6.5 A Formally Verified Defensive Implementation of Sparse Sets as Domains

Let us look at the test function written in WhyML in Fig. 11. The last statement is incorrect since we want to go back to a non-existing previous state. In Why3, when a call to a function is performed, we have to prove that each pre-condition is satisfied. So we need to prove that 2 is in the domain of states, which is not the case here. However, when using the extracted code on the same program, the invariant is broken. A solution to this problem consists in making the undo operation more defensive by testing if its argument refers to a correct state. It implies to keep track of the domain of states in the executable code. For this purpose, we propose to implement the bound sizeD by a *reversible* integer, i.e. a structure containing the current value of the bound and a list of its previous values. This proposition is inspired by the Java implementation of reversible integers in MiniCP [16].

```
let test () : unit =
let a = full_sparse(8) in
remove_sparse 0 a; remove_sparse 6 a;
remove_sparse 1 a; remove_sparse 4 a;
remove_sparse 2 a;
bind_sparse a 5;
assert {2 ∉ (dom states)};    assertion: proved
undo_sparse a 2              pre-condition: proof failed
```

Fig. 11. An Incorrect Program in WhyML

The rint type of reversible integers is defined in Fig. 12. The list of previous values, back, is sorted in increasing order and has no duplicates. So each time an element is removed from the sparse set as domain, the current value in sizeD is pushed in the back list and value is decreased. Each time an element is added, back becomes empty and the value is increased. When undo p is performed, the operation first searches p in back and removes all the values until p in this list before assigning p as the new value of sizeD. In fact the two first actions are done simultaneously, raising an exception if p is not a correct argument.

The WhyML code of the abstract and concrete modules for sparse sets as domains are modified to use reversible integers. To ensure consistency between

```
type rint = { mutable value : int;
              mutable back : list int;
            }
invariant { sorted back && distinct back &&
            forall n. mem n back -> value < n }
```

Fig. 12. WhyML Implementation of Reversible Integers

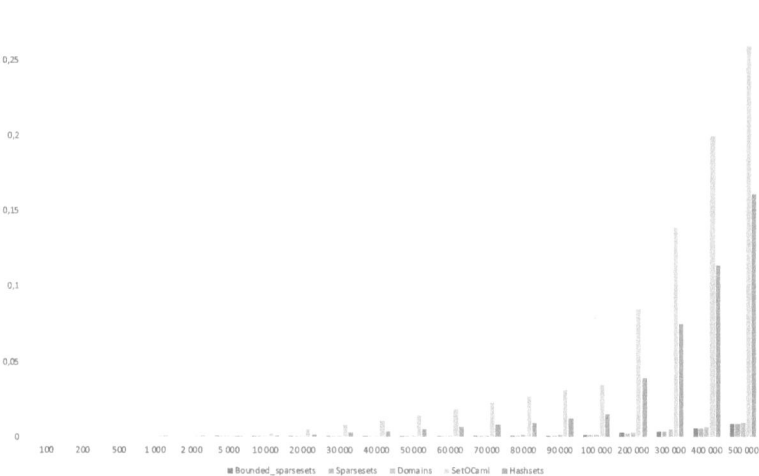

Fig. 13. Comparison of Execution Times on a Naive Implementation of Erathosthenes Sieve Algorithm

sizeD and states, we add the following property in the invariant of the types t and tsparse:

```
forall x. (x = sizeD.value || mem x sizeD.back) <-> x ∈ dom states
```

Proofs of VCs remain automatic.

7   Some Experimentations

We implemented a naive implementation of the Erathosthenes Sieve algorithm following a Web article[5] presenting sparse set implementations in C++, using the OCaml extracted code of three variants of sparse sets: sparse sets *à la* Briggs and Torczon with and without limited capacity and sparse sets as domains. We also implemented this algorithm using the OCaml standard library module Set and an implementation of sets as hash tables[6].

---

[5] https://www.codeproject.com/Articles/859324/Fast-Implementations-of-Sparse-Sets-in-Cplusplus.

[6] https://github.com/backtracking/hashset.

This algorithm performs many insertions, deletions, membership tests and a final call to the operation that computes the cardinality of the sparse set that, at the end, contains the prime numbers up to P, the parameter of the algorithm. In our experimentation whose results are shown on Fig. 13, P varies from one hundred to one million. On the x-axis are the execution times in seconds and on the y-axis the values of P.

On this example sparse sets in their three versions outperform the two set other representations but it is a bit unfair since we are comparing a mutable representation with functional ones. Regarding the three variants, they are equivalent, maintaining the links for removed elements do not impact significantly the execution time.

Our extracted code of sparse sets as domains has been used with a simple sudoku solver originally written in OCaml by Filliâtre[7]. That example intensively uses backtracking and thus the undo operation. It has been evaluated on a large number of sudoku puzzles.

8 Conclusion

In this paper we presented the formal Why3 development for sparse sets and for sparse sets as domains used in constraint solvers. The former refines and extends a partial solution for a more general data structure, sparse arrays, done by Filliâtre and Paskevich some years ago. The latter is a variant of the former, but as far as we know it is the first formalization of this backtrackable data structure that allows the representation of domains of integer variables. We have extracted efficient OCaml code from these formally verified models, which we have experimented on simple test cases, the Erathosthenes Sieve algorithm and a naive sudoku solver. One perspective of this work is the extraction of C code.

The technique used to be able to specify and prove the undo operation has implications for the whole formal development. It allows the use of WhyML and the deductive verification engine of Why3 to prove a property that involves more than a pre- and a post- state, and is close to a dynamic or temporal property.

In the case of very sparse sets or domains, using an array to implement the sparse structure is not optimal in terms of memory space. The data structure could be made more interesting by using another fast access structure, e.g. a hashmap (idea also suggested in [13]). So we could also suggest extending our current work to use such an alternative. It would be more interesting to make this sparse structure a generic parameter of the formalization in order to choose the right implementation à la carte.

As future work, we would also like to integrate sparse sets as domains in a finite domain constraint solver, e.g. in CoqBinFD, a formally verified constraint solver formally verified in Coq [6] or in FaCile, an OCaml constraint library [5].

---

[7] https://github.com/backtracking/ocaml-bazaar/blob/main/sudoku.ml.

Acknowledgements. The author would like to thank the Why3 development team at LMF, Valentin Blot and Jean-Paul Bodeveix, for their interest and helpful comments during an initial presentation of this work. She also thanks the anonymous reviewers for their suggestions and careful reading.

References

1. Abrial, J.-R.: The B-Book. Cambridge University Press, Assigning Programs to Meanings (1996)
2. Abrial, J.-R.: Modeling in Event-B - System and Software Engineering. Cambridge University Press (2010)
3. Aho, A.V., Hopcroft, J.E.: The Design and Analysis of Computer Algorithms, 1st edn. Addison-Wesley Longman Publishing Co., Inc, USA (1974)
4. Briggs, P., Torczon, L.: An efficient representation for sparse sets. LOPLAS **2**(1–4), 59–69 (1993)
5. Brisset, P., Barnier, N.: FaCiLe: a functional constraint library. In: CICLOPS: Colloquium on Implementation of Constraint and LOgic Programming Systems, p. 2001. Paphos, Cyprus (2001)
6. Carlier, M., Dubois, C., Gotlieb, A.: A certified constraint solver over finite domains. In: Formal Methods (FM 2012). volume 7436 of LNCS, pp. 116–131. France, Paris (2012)
7. Cristiá, M., Dubois, C.: Comparing EventB, log and why3 models of sparse sets. In: 35es Journées Francophones des Langages Applicatifs (JFLA 2024). Saint-Jacut-de-la-Mer, France (2024)
8. Cristiá, M., Rossi, G.: {*log*}: set formulas as programs. Rend. Ist. Mat. Univ. Trieste **53**, 24 (2021)
9. Filliâtre, J.-C., Paskevich, A.: Why3 version of the sparse arrays example, the first example of the vacid-0 benchmarks. https://toccata.gitlabpages.inria.fr/toccata/gallery/vacid_0_sparse_array.en.html
10. Filliâtre, J.-C., Paskevich, A.: Why3 - where programs meet provers. In: Felleisen. M., Gardner, P. (eds.) 22nd European Symposium on Programming, ESOP 2013, Held as Part of ETAPS 2013, Rome, Italy, Proceedings, volume 7792 of LNCS, pp. 125–128. Springer (2013)
11. Filliâtre, J.-C., Paskevich A.: Abstraction and genericity in why3. In: Margaria, T., Steffen, B. (eds.) Leveraging Applications of Formal Methods, Verification and Validation: Verification Principles - 9th International Symposium on Leveraging Applications of Formal Methods, ISoLA 2020, Rhodes, Greece, October 20–30, 2020, Proceedings, Part I, volume 12476 of Lecture Notes in Computer Science, pp. 122–142. Springer (2020)
12. Lamport, L.: Specifying Systems. Addison-Wesley, The TLA+ Language and Tools for Hardware and Software Engineers (2002)
13. Le Clément de Saint-Marcq, V., Schaus, P., Solnon, C., Lecoutre C.: Sparse-Sets for domain implementation. In: CP workshop on Techniques foR Implementing Constraint programming Systems (TRICS), pp. 1–10 (2013)
14. Ledein A., Dubois, C.: Facile en coq : vérification formelle des listes d'intervalles. In: 31ème Journées Francophones des Langages Applicatifs (2019)
15. Leino, K.R.M., Moskal, M.: Vacid-0: verification of ample correctness of invariants of data-structures, edition 0. In: Proceedings of Tools and Experiments Workshop at VSTTE (2010)

16. Michel, L., Schaus, P., Van Hentenryck, P.: Minicp: a lightweight solver for constraint programming. Math. Program. Comput. **13**(1), 133–184 (2021)
17. Schaus, P., Landtsheer, R.D.: Oscar user-guide (2016). http://oscarlib.org
18. Schwartz, J.T., Dewar, R.B.K., Dubinsky, E., Schonberg, E.: Programming with Sets - An Introduction to SETL. Texts and Monographs in Computer Science. Springer (1986)

POLYSAT: Word-level Bit-vector Reasoning in Z3

Jakob Rath[1]($\boxtimes$)(iD), Clemens Eisenhofer[1](iD), Daniela Kaufmann[1](iD),
Nikolaj Bjørner[2](iD), and Laura Kovács[1]($\boxtimes$)(iD)

[1] TU Wien, Vienna, Austria
{jakob.rath,clemens.eisenhofer,daniela.kaufmann,
laura.Kovacs}@tuwien.ac.at
[2] Microsoft Research, Redmond, USA
nbjorner@microsoft.com

Abstract. POLYSAT is a word-level decision procedure supporting bit-precise SMT reasoning over polynomial arithmetic with large bit-vector operations. Addressing challenges of verified software, POLYSAT integrates the theoretical development of SMT-based calculi with a proof of concept implementation and empirical evaluation. The POLYSAT calculus extends conflict-driven clause learning modulo theories with two key components: (i) a bit-vector plugin to the equality graph, and (ii) a theory solver for bit-vector arithmetic with non-linear polynomials. POLYSAT implements dedicated procedures to extract bit-vector intervals from polynomial inequalities. For conflict analysis and resolution, POLYSAT comes with on-demand lemma generation over non-linear bit-vector arithmetic. POLYSAT is integrated into the SMT solver Z3 and has applications in model checking and smart contract verification where bit-blasting techniques on multipliers/divisions do not scale.

Keywords: SMT Solving · Bit-vector Theory · Word-level Reasoning · Software Verification

1 Introduction

Bit-vector reasoning plays a central role in applications of system verification, enabling for example efficient bounded model checking [11], bit-precise memory handling [23], or proving safety of decentralized financial transactions [1]. Although one may argue that, because bit-vectors are bounded, bit-vector reasoning is simpler than proving arithmetic properties over the integers or reals, showing (un)satisfiability of bit-vector problems is inherently expensive due to complex arithmetic operations over large bit-widths [20].

Related Works. State-of-the-art satisfiability modulo theories (SMT) solvers handle bit-vector operations by *bit-blasting* [21], i.e., translating bit-vector formulas into propositional ones that can be solved by ordinary propositional satisfiability

(SAT) solvers. Practically all state-of-the-art SMT solvers supporting the bit-vector theory contain a bit-blasting solver [2,10,13,16,25,28]. While the core idea of translating bit-vector operations to SAT formulas is quite natural, the different solvers vary considerably in the specific details of this translation and related techniques such as pre-processing and using over- and under-approximations to simplify solving.

Yet, the bit-blasting method performs poorly when multiplications are involved. As a result, several different strategies have been investigated in attempts to overcome this issue.

Layered techniques [7,18] first apply several layers of cheap but incomplete word-level procedures and then fall back to lazy bit-blasting; this way, only the relevant parts of the input where none of the incomplete procedures apply needs to be bit-blasted.

Another technique puts an abstraction-refinement loop on top of a bit-blasting solver [30], abstracting bit-vector multiplication, division, and remainder operations as uninterpreted functions. These operations are then refined incrementally by adding lemmas to the solver (somewhat similar as in our Sect. 6), falling back to standard bit-blasting when necessary.

In contrast, purely word-level techniques have been developed as well. In a method called *Int-Blasting* [36], bit-vector constraints are translated into non-linear integer arithmetic constraints.

The model-constructing satisfiability calculus (MCSAT) [26] has been proposed as an alternative to CDCL(T). In MCSAT, Boolean and theory decisions are interleaved on a shared trail. Propagation and conflict explanation is handled by theory-specific plugins. Bit-vector plugins for MCSAT [17,35] generate word-level explanations for supported fragments of the bit-vector language and fall back to bit-level explanations otherwise. Quantifier elimination algorithms [19] have been developed for certain fragments of bit-vector logic, which may serve as a basis of conflict explanation.

The solver WOMBIT [33] uses a hybrid approach: it employs word-level propagation during search, but then generates justifications based on individual bits during conflict resolution.

Stochastic local search [14,27,29] has been developed to quickly find models for satisfiable instances, but in general, does not terminate for unsatisfiable problems.

PolySAT – Our Contribution. In this paper, we propose POLYSAT, a *word-level reasoning procedure* integrated into SMT solving as a theory solver. POLYSAT is based on conflict-driven clause learning modulo theories (CDCL(T)), providing *an alternative to bit-blasting.*

While our work builds on previous research on bit-vector slicing [8], forbidden intervals [17], and fixing bits [35], we extend these efforts as follows. We generalize forbidden intervals to non-unit coefficients (Sect. 5), while in [17] forbidden intervals are extracted only from constraints with unit coefficients. We further introduce theory lemmas to partially handle non-linear conflicts (Sect. 6), whereas in [17] such conflicts are deferred to bit-blasting. Finally, POLYSAT uses intervals to track viable values and detect conflicts, whereas in [17], forbidden intervals are used only to construct a lemma after a conflict has been detected, and in [35], viable values are tracked by a combination of fixed bits and a single interval consisting of a lower and upper bound. We integrate bit-vector slicing from [8] and [17] as a plugin into the main e-graph of the SMT solver (Sect. 3.1).

In our setting, we consider bit-vectors as elements of the ring $\mathbb{Z}/2^w\mathbb{Z}$. Informally, arithmetical operations on bit-vectors can be seen as the respective integer operations, where the result is evaluated "$\mod 2^w$". Yet, due to modulo/bounded arithmetic, many properties of the integers (such as, there is no maximal element and no zero-divisors) do not hold over bit-vectors. Nevertheless, with PolySAT we support bit-vector arithmetic without bit-blasting.

PolySAT – Illustrative Example. We illustrate the benefits of PolySAT using the next example.

Example 1. Consider the bit-vector constraints with large bit-width w:

$$xy + y >_\mathsf{u} y + 3 \qquad 1 = 3x + 6yz + 3z^2$$
$$6 = 2y + z \qquad 0 = (2y + 1) \mathbin{\&} x$$

where "$\&$" denotes the bit-wise *and* operation and $>_\mathsf{u}$ refers to unsigned comparison. PolySAT proves this set of bit-vector constraints to be unsat, without using bit-blasting as follows.

We initially guess the assignment $x = 0$, simplifying the first constraint to $y >_\mathsf{u} y + 3$. We pick the assignment $y = 2^w - 2$ which is feasible w.r.t. the inequality. Hence, the constraint $6 = 2y + z$ simplifies to $z = 10$, which conflicts with the constraint $1 = 3x + 6yz + 3z^2$. We backtrack, apply variable elimination upon y on the two equality constraints, and learn the *new equation* $3x + 18z = 1$. From the bit-wise $\&$-constraint, we derive that x is even, as $2y + 1$ is odd. This conflicts with the learned equation, as the learned equation $3x + 18z = 1$ implies that x is odd. Hence, PolySAT concludes that the given constraints are unsat.

PolySAT – Main Improvements. With PolySAT, we bring the following main improvements to word-level reasoning over bit-vectors.

- We adjust the concept of forbidden intervals [17] to track viable values in PolySAT (Sect. 4);
- We extract bit-vector intervals from polynomial (non-linear) inequalities (Sect. 5);
- We introduce lemmas on-demand for detecting and resolving non-linear conflicts in PolySAT (Sect. 6).
- We implement PolySAT directly in the SMT solver Z3 [25] and evaluate our work on challenging examples (Sect. 7).

Paper Outline. We discuss required preliminaries in Sect. 2 and provide an overview of PolySAT in Sect. 3. We describe our main methodological contributions in Sects. 4–6 and present our experimental evaluation in Sect. 7. Section 8 concludes our work.

2   Preliminaries

For a given number of bits $w > 0$, we consider bit-vectors of size w as elements of the ring $\mathbb{Z}/2^w\mathbb{Z}$ (algebraic representation), or equivalently as strings of length w over $\{0,1\}$ (binary representation). Throughout the paper, we write w for the size of related bit-vectors, when it is clear from the context. In other cases, we denote the size of x by $|x|$ explicitly.

For conversion from bit-vectors to integers, unless explicitly stated otherwise, we default to the *unsigned* interpretation of bit-vectors, i.e., choose the representatives $\{0, 1, \ldots, 2^w - 1\}$ for elements of $\mathbb{Z}/2^w\mathbb{Z}$. Negative constants such as -1 stand for their equivalent $2^w - 1$.

We write $x \leq_u y$ for unsigned comparison of bit-vectors, and use $x \leq_s y$ to denote signed comparison. For simplicity of notation, we use "$=$" for both object-level equality and meta-level equality.

The basic building blocks of POLYSAT constraints are *polynomials*, i.e., multiplications and additions of bit-vector variables and constants. We emphasize bit-vector multiplication by writing "$\cdot$" explicitly.

We write $x[i]$ for the i-th bit of the bit-vector x, where $x[0]$ denotes the least significant bit. Let $x \mathbin{+\!\!\!+} y$ denote the concatenation of x and y.

We write $x[h{:}l]$, with $0 \leq l \leq h < w$, for the *sub-slice* ranging from bit h to bit l inclusively, i.e., $x[h{:}l] = x[h] \mathbin{+\!\!\!+} x[h-1] \mathbin{+\!\!\!+} \ldots \mathbin{+\!\!\!+} x[l]$. We call the sub-slices $x[i{:}0]$ the *prefixes* of x.

We use half-open *wrapping* intervals over the domain $\mathbb{Z}/2^w\mathbb{Z}$. That is, for $l > h$ we define $[l; h[:= [0; h[\cup [l; 2^w[$. Then, $t \in [l; h[$ is equivalent to the bit-vector inequality $t - l <_u h - l$.

3   POLYSAT in a Nutshell

POLYSAT serves as a decision procedure for bit-vector constraints and is developed as a theory solver within the SMT solver Z3 [25]. An overview of the POLYSAT architecture is given in Fig. 1, with further details on key ingredients in Sects. 4–6.

In a nutshell, POLYSAT consists of two inter-connected components that interact for theory solving in an SMT setting:

1. A *bit-vector plugin to the equality graph, in short e-graph* [12,34]. This plugin handles structural constraints that involve multiple bit-widths (concatenation, extraction) and determines canonical sub-slices of bit-vectors. The POLYSAT e-graph plugin also propagates assigned values across bit-vector slices.
2. A *theory solver*, which handles the remaining constraints by translating them into *polynomial constraints* (Fig. 2) and builds on information from the e-graph plugin to search for a satisfiable assignment (Sects. 4–6).

From its e-graph, POLYSAT receives Boolean assignments to bit-vector constraints, and equality propagations between bit-vector terms. In return, the theory solver of POLYSAT produces a satisfying assignment, or a conflicting subset

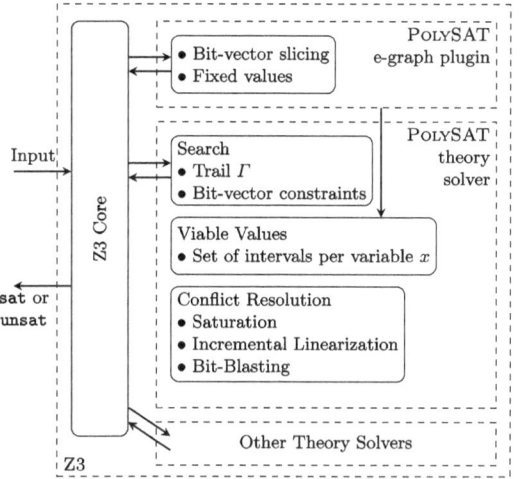

Fig. 1. PolySAT Integration

$p \leq_u q$	unsigned inequality
$\Omega^*(p,q)$	multiplicative overflow
$x = p \,\&\, q$	bit-wise *and*
$x = p \mid q$	bit-wise *or*
$x = p \ll q$	left shift
$x = p \gg q$	logical right shift
$x = p \gg_a q$	arithmetic right shift

Fig. 2. Primitive Constraints

$$p <_u q \quad \rightsquigarrow \quad \neg(q \leq_u p)$$
$$p \leq_s q \quad \rightsquigarrow \quad p + 2^{w-1} \leq_u q + 2^{w-1}$$
$$p = q \quad \rightsquigarrow \quad p - q \leq_u 0$$
$$\Omega^+(p,q) \quad \rightsquigarrow \quad p + q <_u p$$
$$p[i] \quad \rightsquigarrow \quad 2^{w-1} \leq_u 2^{w-i-1}p$$
$$p - q \quad \rightsquigarrow \quad p + (2^w - 1)q$$
$$\sim p \quad \rightsquigarrow \quad -p - 1$$

Fig. 3. Derived Constraints

of the received constraints. We next discuss these two components, and then focus on the theory solving aspects of PolySAT in Sects. 4–6.

3.1 E-Graph Plugin

In SMT solving, an e-graph [12,34] is typically shared between theory solvers. The primary purpose of the e-graph is to infer equalities that follow from congruence reasoning. For PolySAT, the e-graph is extended with theory reasoning for bit-vectors. Theory reasoning is dispatched when the e-graph merges two terms of bit-vector sort. PolySAT determines the bits of variables that are fixed by certain types of constraints ("fixed bits") and performs constant propagation over bit-vector extraction and concatenation. Furthermore, the PolySAT e-graph establishes equalities between bit-vector ranges. For example, it infers that $x[5:4] = x[1:0]$ from the equation $x[5:2] = x[3:0]$.

We note that congruence reasoning for bit-vectors was also considered in [6, 8,24]. Moreover, e-graphs are also used for constant propagation in [17]. The PolySAT integration of theory plugins to the e-graph structure is generic and not specific to bit-vectors.

3.2 Theory Solver

The *propositional search* is driven by the CDCL(T) core of the SMT solver [4,31]. PolySAT receives Boolean assignments to bit-vector constraints and equality propagations between bit-vector terms. Both of them are translated into primitive constraints (cf. Figure 2) and tracked by the *trail* Γ. PolySAT maintains the invariant that each element of Γ is justified by previous elements, and that each constraint and variable is assigned at most once in Γ.

Value search in POLYSAT assigns viable values (see Sect. 4) to bit-vector variables, which are communicated back to the SMT solver core as variable assignment constraints.

Constraints. Overall, POLYSAT fully supports the standardized bit-vector logic of SMT-LIB [3]. Extraction and concatenation are handled by POLYSAT's e-graph plugin, while other bit-vector constraints are passed to its theory solver. Figure 2 depicts the *primitive constraints*, where p, q are bit-vector polynomials and x is a bit-vector variable. Other constraints are either internally reduced to primitive constraints as shown in Fig. 3, or axiomatized upfront.

For example, to internalize the (unsigned) division $x \,/\, y$, POLYSAT introduces fresh variables $q := x \,/\, y$ and $r := x \,\%\, y$ for the quotient and remainder, respectively. The main axiom is $x = qy + r$, but for correctness in bit-vector logic, four more axioms are required:

$$\neg\Omega^*(q,y) \qquad\qquad y \neq 0 \;\rightarrow\; r <_\mathsf{u} y$$
$$\neg\Omega^+(qy,r) \qquad\qquad y = 0 \;\rightarrow\; q = -1$$

where $\neg\Omega^+(qy,r)$ means that the addition $qy + r$ does not overflow, which can be implemented, e.g., as the constraint $qy \leq_\mathsf{u} -r - 1$.

Constraints of the form $x = n$, where x is a variable and n is a bit-vector constant, are called *variable assignments*. Bit-vector terms p and constraints c can be evaluated w.r.t. the current trail Γ, that is, we substitute the variable assignments in Γ into p and c, respectively, and simplify. As a shorthand, we write $\widehat{p}$ for the evaluation of p under the current trail.

POLYSAT uses rewriting to simplify different syntactic forms of equivalent constraints. In particular, we normalize several forms of equations that may appear in modular arithmetic. For instance, the constraints $p \leq_\mathsf{u} 0$, $p <_\mathsf{u} 1$, and $2^w - 1 \leq_\mathsf{u} p - 1$, are all normalized to $p = 0$.

Constraint Solving. The POLYSAT theory solver uses a waterfall model of refinements to generate lemmas on demand, using the following steps:

1. *Propagation*: Value propagation is triggered when a variable is assigned a value (Sect. 4.1).
2. *Viable Interval Conflict*: If propagation tightens the feasible intervals of a variable to the empty set, the solver yields an interval conflict (Sect. 4.3).
3. *Case Split on Viable Candidates*: If no further propagation is possible, and there are no interval conflicts, the solver picks a value for the next unassigned variable, if any. It produces a literal $x = n$ for the CDCL solver to case split on, with a preference to the phase $x = n$ over $x \neq n$. The constant n is chosen to be outside the ranges of infeasible intervals stored for x so far (Sect. 4.2).
4. *Saturation Lemmas*: Saturation lemmas let us propagate consequences from non-linear constraints (Sect. 6.1).
5. *Incremental Linearization*: Our solver includes incremental linearization rules for the cases where variables are 0, 1, −1, or powers of two (Sect. 6.2).

6. *Bit-blasting*: As a final resort, POLYSAT admits bit-blasting rules (Sect. 6.3).

The first three steps above (steps 1, 2, 3) operate on linear constraints, or rather, a *linear abstraction* of the original constraints, where non-linear monomials are treated as variables themselves. If no conflicts arise from the linear abstraction, then any conflicting non-linear constraints are handled by the latter stages (steps 4, 5, 6 above).

A conflict at any stage will cause POLYSAT to return a conflict lemma to the SMT solver core, which will then backtrack and continue with search. When control is passed to POLYSAT the next time, theory solving in POLYSAT will begin again in the above step 1 of constraint solving.

4 Tracking Viable Values

In the following, we discuss the key ingredients of the theory solving component of POLYSAT. A crucial part of the POLYSAT theory solver tracks for each bit-vector variable x an over-approximation of the set of feasible values under the current trail Γ, which we call the *viable* values of x. Specifically, the set of viable values is represented as a set of *forbidden intervals*, each of which excludes a certain range of values of x, and is justified by constraints in the current trail Γ.

In POLYSAT, we adapt forbidden intervals from [17] and use intervals for propagating and querying viable values of variables (Sects. 4.1–4.2), and resolving respective conflicts (Sect. 4.3). Our approach extends [17] by computing intervals when the coefficient of x is not a power of two (Section 5.1), or when the coefficients are different on both sides of an inequality (Section 5.2).

4.1 Value Propagation

POLYSAT extracts forbidden intervals from inequalities and overflow constraints c that are linear in x under the current trail Γ. Formally, we determine an interval $[l; u[$ and side conditions $c_1, \ldots, c_n$ that hold under Γ such that

$$c \wedge c_1 \wedge \cdots \wedge c_n \implies x \notin [l; u[.$$

Intervals are ordered by their starting points, and we drop intervals that are fully contained in other intervals. Section 5 explains how intervals are obtained from constraints.

Value propagation in POLYSAT is triggered when a variable is assigned a value, or in other words, the solver is presented with a literal $x = n$, where n is a value. Propagation is limited to linear occurrences of variables. For example, if x is assigned 2, then from $x + y \geq_u 10$, the non viable intervals for y are updated to $y \notin [-2; 8[$. On the other hand, for $xz + y \geq_u 10$, where x occurs in a non-linear term, there is no propagation. Non-linear propagation in POLYSAT is currently side-stepped because we noticed that it produced very weak lemmas from viable interval conflicts. Non-linear conflicts are therefore handled separately, see Sect. 6.

4.2 Viable Value Query

To find a viable value for variable x, we collect the forbidden intervals $\mathcal{I}$ over the prefixes $x[k{:}0]$ of x for $0 \leq k < w$. In this context, iff an interval $I \in \mathcal{I}$ is an interval for $x[k{:}0]$, we say I *has bit-width* $k+1$. In addition, we consider intervals for variables that are equivalent to a prefix of x, as determined by the current state of the e-graph.

Algorithm 1: PolySAT Viable Value Query

Input   : Set of forbidden intervals $\mathcal{I}$, set C of constraints
Output : Viable value x_0, or a conflict

1 $x_0 \leftarrow x_{prev}$ ▷ Start at previous viable value
2 $\mathcal{J} \leftarrow \langle\rangle$ ▷ Justification (sequence of visited intervals)
3 **loop**
4   **while** $\exists I \in \mathcal{I}$ *such that* $x_0 \in I$ **do**
5   Choose such an $I \in \mathcal{I}$ with smallest bit-width
6         $\mathcal{J} \leftarrow \langle \mathcal{J}; I \rangle$
7         $x_0 \leftarrow forward(x_0, I)$
8   **if** $isConflict(\mathcal{J})$ **then return** Conflict $\mathcal{J}$
9   **if** x_0 *does not violate any* $c \in C$ **then return** x_0
10     $\mathcal{I} \leftarrow \mathcal{I} \cup \{computeInterval(C, x_0)\}$

In addition to forbidden intervals, we keep track of the set C of constraints that are linear in x. We then invoke Algorithm 1 to either find a value for x or detect a conflict. We resolve limitations of [17] by using intervals to track viable values and detect conflicts in Algorithm 1 as follows.

Algorithm 1 starts out with the previous viable value x_{prev} of x, initially set to 0. Then, in the loop of Algorithm 1, we check whether any of the known intervals $\mathcal{I}$ contain the current candidate value x_0 of x. If that is not the case, then the current value x_0 is compatible with the intervals in $\mathcal{I}$. We additionally test x_0 for admissibility against the set C of constraints (line 9 of Algorithm 1). If none of these constraints are violated, the candidate value x_0 is returned as viable value for x. Otherwise (line 10 of Algorithm 1), $computeInterval(C, x_0)$ extracts a new interval that covers x_0 (cf. Sect. 5) and the search for a viable value of x continues. If, on the other hand, the current value x_0 of x is contained in some forbidden interval, we choose an interval I of minimal bit-width among these (line 5 of Algorithm 1) and record it in the list $\mathcal{J}$ of justifications (line 6 of Algorithm 1).

The candidate value x_0 of x is updated to $forward(x_0, I)$, the first value after x_0 that is not covered by I (line 7 of Algorithm 1). If a conflict is detected (line 8 of Algorithm 1), the justifications $\mathcal{J}$ are returned for further processing (see Sect. 4.3).

The following example illustrates the execution of Algorithm 1.

Example 2. Assume PolySAT needs to determine a viable value for the variable y where the set of initially known intervals $\mathcal{I}$ is empty, the set of constraints C consists of the three constraints c_1, c_2, c_3 listed below, and the trail contains the assignment $x = 11$.   To find a viable value, PolySAT invokes

	Constraint	Equivalent Interval	Concrete Interval
c_1	$4 \leq_u y$	$y \notin [0; 4[$	$y \notin [0; 4[$
c_2	$y \leq_u 15$	$y \notin [16; 0[$	$y \notin [16; 0[$
c_3	$x + 3 \leq_u y + 5$	$y \notin [-5; x - 2[$ when $x + 3 \neq 0$	$y \notin [-5; 9[$

Algorithm 1. As this is the first invocation, we begin with $y_0 = 0$. The condition of the while loop (line 4) is trivially false. Since constraint c_1 is false for $y = 0$, we extract the interval $[0; 4[$ as described in Sect. 5 and add it to $\mathcal{I}$ (line 10).

In the next iteration of the algorithm's outer loop (line 3), we enter the while loop body with the interval $I = [0; 4[$; advancing y_0 to the value 4 and recording I in the justifications $\mathcal{J}$. This time, we find y_0 violates constraint c_3 (line 9). As before, we extract the interval $[-5; 9[$ and store it in $\mathcal{I}$.

In the third iteration of the outer loop (line 3), we advance y_0 to 9 and record $[-5; 9[$ in the set of justifications $\mathcal{J}$. Further, we discover that $y = 9$ does not contradict any of the relevant constraints C (line 9) and the algorithm terminates. We conclude that 9 is a viable value for y.

Consider now a subsequent invocation of Algorithm 1 for y with the additional constraint c_4 (listed below), i.e., $C = \{c_1, c_2, c_3, c_4\}$. This situation may happen in PolySAT if a conflict occurs in the branch with $y = 9$ and c_4 is then derived by conflict resolution. Note that the previously discovered viable

	Constraint	Equivalent Interval	Concrete Interval
c_4	$y - 12 \leq_u y - x + 4$	$y \notin [x - 4; 12[$	$y \notin [7; 12[$

value now serves as starting point for the search, i.e., the second invocation of Algorithm 1 begins with $y_0 = 9$. We notice that c_4 is violated for this value of y, compute the interval $[7; 12[$, and advance to $y_0 = 12$. Now, none of the constraints are violated and the algorithm returns the viable value 12.

Finally, consider a third invocation of Algorithm 1 for y with the additional constraint $c_5 \colon y + 1 \leq_u 11$, which is equivalent to the interval $y \notin [11; -1[$. This time, the search starts at $y_0 = 12$. We find, in the listed order, the intervals $[11; -1[, [-5; 9[, [7; 12[$ and finally, $[11; -1[$ again. At this point, a conflict is detected, justified by the listed intervals. The algorithm terminates and returns the justification for the conflict for further processing.

Note that, while constraint c_2 is relevant for y, it has been skipped in the algorithm because its interval has been covered by other constraints.

Remark 1. In the above Example 2, we obtained the intervals $[0; 4[$ and $[-5; 9[$. The former is fully contained in the latter and thus unnecessary to determine the viable value. In our implementation, we prune such subsumed intervals from the set $\mathcal{I}$ and from the justifications $\mathcal{J}$.

4.3   Interval Conflict

We detect conflicts by examining the list of justifications $\mathcal{J}$ after appending a new interval I to $\mathcal{J}$. The condition *isConflict*$(\mathcal{J})$ in Algorithm 1 is true iff the latest interval I has already been visited previously, and no interval of larger bit-width has occurred in between. Let $I_1, \ldots, I_{n+1}$ denote this subsequence of intervals, where $I_1 = I_{n+1} = I$, and let $I_i = [l_i; h_i[$. To block the current assignment to x, POLYSAT creates a conflict lemma from $I_1, \ldots, I_{n+1}$ and reports it to its SMT core. For simplicity, we only explain here the case where all intervals have the same bit-width.

The POLYSAT conflict lemma is used to capture the following fact: the union of $I_1, \ldots, I_n$ covers the full domain $\mathbb{Z}/w\mathbb{Z}$, and the intervals have been chosen such that each upper bound h_i in contained in the next interval I_{i+1}. In other words, as long as $h_i \in I_{i+1}$ holds, for all i, and the intervals are valid for x, there can be no feasible value for x in POLYSAT. While the POLYSAT conflict lemma is similar to the one of [17], we note that [17] succinctly represents constraints $h_i \in I_{i+1}$ when multiple bit-widths are involved; this is not the case with POLYSAT as we avoid using extract-expressions.

Since the constraints $h_i \in I_{i+1}$ in POLYSAT do not contain x itself, they are useful for formulating a conflict lemma. Let C_i denote the set consisting of the constraint and side conditions of I_i. Then, the POLYSAT conflict lemma is

$$\bigwedge_{i=1}^{n} C_i \wedge \bigwedge_{i=1}^{n} h_i \in I_{i+1} \implies \bot.$$

To illustrate the idea of conflict lemma generation in POLYSAT, consider three intervals $[l_1; h_1[, [l_2; h_2[, [l_3; h_3[$ whose concrete evaluation under the current trail Γ covers the full domain by forming the following configuration:

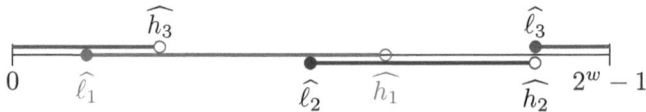

Assuming the three intervals are justified by constraints C_1, C_2, C_3, respectively, the POLYSAT conflict lemma is

$$\bigwedge C \wedge h_1 \in [l_2; h_2[\wedge h_2 \in [l_3; h_3[\wedge h_3 \in [l_1; h_1[\implies \bot,$$

where $C := C_1 \cup C_2 \cup C_3$.

5   Computing Intervals

We now describe how forbidden intervals are extracted from a constraint $c \in C$ that is linear in the variable x under consideration. Intervals may be computed on demand, relative to a given candidate value (sample point) x_0 of x: the goal is then to find a maximal interval around x_0 of x-values that are excluded by c. In practice, we note the intervals are often not strictly maximal, but as large as reasonably possible to compute.

5.1   Linear Inequality with Equal Coefficients

Given the inequality constraint $px + q \leq_u rx + s$ that is linear in x. In the cases where either p or r evaluate to 0 or both to the same value a, the inequality constraint is equivalent to an interval constraint [17], according to the following table, and subject to side conditions $p = \widehat{p}$ and $r = \widehat{r}$:

Constraint under Γ	Forbidden Interval	Condition
$ax + \widehat{q} \leq_u \widehat{s}$	$ax \notin [s - q + 1; -q[$	$s \neq -1$
$\widehat{q} \leq_u ax + \widehat{s}$	$ax \notin [-s; q - s[$	$q \neq 0$
$ax + \widehat{q} \leq_u ax + \widehat{s}$	$ax \notin [-s; -q[$	$q \neq s$

Assume we have $ax \in [l; h[$. Yet, we want to extract an interval on x, rather than on ax.

Case $a = \pm 1$: The case $a = 1$ trivially leads to such an interval. In the case $a = -1$ (i.e., $2^w - 1$), the transformation $-x \in [l; h[\Leftrightarrow x \in [1 - h; 1 - l[$ is applied.

Case $a = \alpha 2^k$ (reducing the bit-width): Consider the case where a is divisible by 2^k for some $k > 0$. Due to the factor 2^k, the upper k bits of x do not influence the value of the constraint. In this case, we consider an interval for the prefix $x[w - k - 1{:}0]$ of x:

$$\alpha 2^k x \notin [l; h[\iff \begin{cases} \alpha x[w - k - 1{:}0] \notin [l'; h'[& \text{if } l' \neq h' \\ 0 \notin [l; h[& \text{otherwise} \end{cases}$$

where $\beta' := \lceil \frac{\beta}{2^k} \rceil \bmod 2^{w-k}$ for $\beta \in \{l, h\}$.

Other values of a: For other values of a, in general, multiple disjoint intervals exist. We extract intervals around a sample point x_0 on demand, i.e., given concrete values $a, x_0, l, h \in \mathbb{Z}/2^w\mathbb{Z}$ such that $ax_0 \in [l; h[$, the task is to compute the maximal x-interval $[x_l; x_h[$ such that $ax \in [l; h[$ for all $x \in [x_l; x_h[$. To compute x_l and x_h, we move the problem into the integers $\mathbb{Z}$ and work with non-wrapping intervals. Operations until the end of this subsection are therefore to be understood as operations in $\mathbb{Z}$.

Let w be a fixed bit-width and let $m := 2^w$. Assume values $a, x_0, l, h \in \mathbb{Z}$ are given such that $1 \le a < m$, $-m < l \le h < m$, and $ax_0 \bmod m \in [l; h]$. Furthermore, the length of the interval should be less than m, i.e., $h - l + 1 < m$ (otherwise the computation is unnecessary because the corresponding modular interval covers the whole domain). The goal is to find the minimal x_l and the maximal x_h such that $ax \bmod m \in [l; h]$ for all $x \in [x_l; x_h]$.

Let $k_0 \in \mathbb{Z}$ such that $l \le ax_0 + k_0 m \le h$. To simplify notation, define $\langle x \rangle := x + k_0 m$. The initial configuration is illustrated by the following diagram:

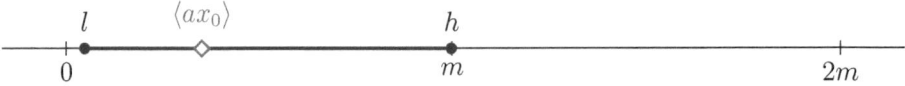

Since we are ultimately interested in the modular interval $[l; h] \bmod m$ over $\mathbb{Z}/m\mathbb{Z}$, we consider the set of all representatives of elements of that interval, i.e., the union of $[l; h] + im$ for all $i \in \mathbb{Z}$, as depicted in the following diagram.

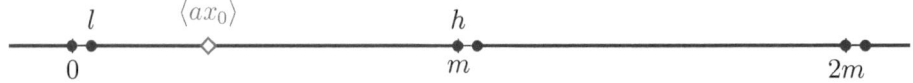

The underlying idea of our procedure is to look at each interval representative $[l; h] + im$ separately (intuitively, as a region where no overflow occurs) and take advantage of periodicity after each overflow.

In the first step, we compute the minimal x_l' and the maximal x_h' such that $l \le \langle ax \rangle \le h$ for all $x \in [x_l'; x_h']$. Intuitively, $[x_l'; x_h']$ is the maximal x-interval around x_0 such that no overflow occurs among the corresponding multiples of a.

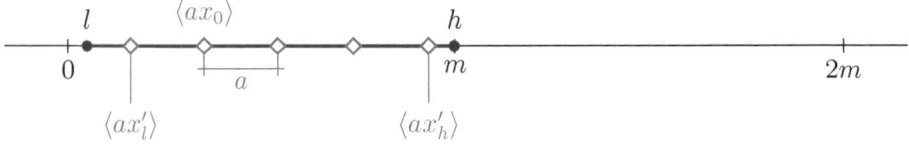

However, the interval $[x_l'; x_h']$ is often far from optimal, causing repeated queries over the same constraint in Algorithm 1. In case of the upper bound, this means that $\langle a(x_h' + 1) \rangle$ is contained in the next interval representative $[l; h] + m$. The following diagram illustrates the multiples of a across several interval representatives.

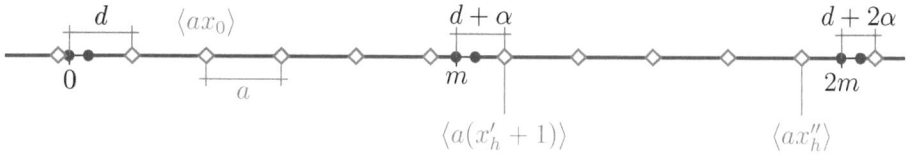

The situation in the second interval $[l; h] + m$ is very similar to the initial setting. However, the multiples of a (depicted by red diamonds) have shifted by some amount α relative to the interval.

In the example illustrated in the diagrams we have $\alpha < 0$, i.e., with each overflow, the multiples of a drift to the left (relative to the interval). With different parameters, $\alpha = 0$ (no drift) and $\alpha > 0$ (drift to the right) are also possible.

For $\alpha < 0$, we keep overflowing until the leftmost multiple of a drifts outside the interval. For $\alpha > 0$, similarly for the rightmost multiple of a (in this case, the final considered interval will be irregular in the sense that it contains one fewer multiple of a).

In case $\alpha = 0$, the situation for each interval representative is exactly the same, and we conclude no upper bound x_h exists (which means the final x-interval over $\mathbb{Z}/m\mathbb{Z}$ will be the full domain).

We have described our method to compute the upper bound x_h. The lower bound x_l can be computed analogously. In fact, PolySAT reduces the computation of x_l to the computation of x_h by mirroring the initial configuration and the result across 0. Let f denote the procedure for calculating x_h, i.e., $x_h = f(x_0, a, l, h, m)$. Then $x_l = -f(-x_0, a, -h, -l, \text{ } m)$.

Even though this method works well in practice, some limitations remain. The interval extension ends as soon as one of the red diamonds is outside the blue interval. This is by specification, but it does mean that this method is only helpful when the gap between blue intervals (i.e., $m - (h - l)$) is less than the distance between red diamonds (i.e., a).

5.2   Linear Inequality with Different Coefficients

Consider an inequality c of the form $px + q \leq_u rx + s$ with $\hat{p} \neq \hat{r}$. Here, we need to find the largest x-interval around a sample point x_0 where c is satisfied. As Fig. 4a shows for an example, the corresponding problem is easily solved over infinite domains, such as rationals, by computing the intersection point of the left- and right-hand side of the inequality. The interval then extends from the intersection point towards infinity.

However, in modular arithmetic, the left-hand side and the right-hand side of c do not represent continuous lines; instead, they wrap around at 2^w as seen in Fig. 4b. As such, the solution is not necessarily a single interval; the desired intervals extend from an intersection point to the next wraparound point. PolySAT computes and returns the interval containing x_0. In some configurations, the gap between one interval to the next (i.e., between the green lines in Fig. 4b) does not contain an integer, which means the obtained x-interval is not maximal. This method works best when the coefficients $\widehat{p}$ and $\widehat{q}$ of x are near 0 or 2^w.

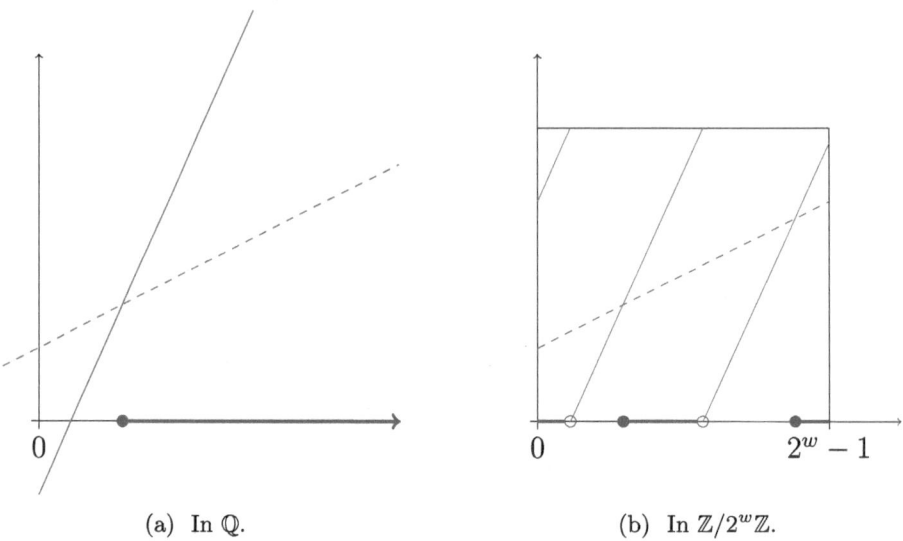

(a) In $\mathbb{Q}$.   (b) In $\mathbb{Z}/2^w\mathbb{Z}$.

Fig. 4. Example for extracting intervals from an inequality constraint $px + q \leq_u rx + s$ with different variable coefficients. The blue dashed line plots $\widehat{p}(Color figure online)x + \widehat{q}$, and the red continuous line is $\widehat{r}x + \widehat{s}$.

Computing Intersection and Wraparound Points. In order to work out the above intuition more precisely, consider the inequality c of the form $px + q \leq_u rx + s$ with $p, q, r, s \in \mathbb{Z}/2^w\mathbb{Z}$ such that $p \neq 0$, $r \neq 0$ and $p \neq r$. Let $x_0 \in \mathbb{Z}/2^w\mathbb{Z}$ be a sample value that violates the constraint, i.e., such that $(px_0 + q) \bmod 2^w > (rx_0 + s) \bmod 2^w$ (to avoid confusion, we write "mod" operations in this section explicitly).

The goal is to find a maximal x-interval around x_0 whose elements all violate the constraint, i.e., we want to find the minimal x_l and the maximal x_h such that $x_l \leq x_0 \leq x_h$ and $(px + q) \bmod 2^w > (rx + s) \bmod 2^w$ for all $x \in [x_l; x_h]$.

In the following, we explain our method for extracting such intervals, however, we cannot yet guarantee to obtain a maximal interval in all cases. As illustrated in Fig. 4, we extrapolate the left-hand side (LHS) and the right-hand side (RHS) of the constraint using standard arithmetic until the next overflow point, and extract the maximal interval that can be obtained without overflow.

Let us define the abbreviations $a := (px_0 + q) \bmod 2^w$ and $b := (rx_0 + s) \bmod 2^w$. From now on, we view p, q, r, s, a, b as values over the rationals $\mathbb{Q}$ by choosing the representative in the interval $[0; 2^w[$.

To compute a safe upper bound $x_h = x_0 + \delta_h$, we find the maximal $\delta_h \in \mathbb{Z}$ satisfying the following conditions:

- $\delta_h \geq 0$, i.e., it should be an *upper* bound,
- $\forall x.(0 \leq x \leq \delta_h \rightarrow 2^w > a + px > b + rx \geq 0)$, i.e., the LHS and RHS do not overflow within the interval and the constraint is violated for all values,
- $x_0 + \delta_h < 2^w$, i.e., the upper bound does not overflow.

After several transformations, we obtain the formula

$$\delta_h = \min\left(\left\{2^w - x_0, \lceil\frac{2^w - a}{p}\rceil\right\} \cup \left\{\lceil\frac{a-b}{r-p}\rceil \,\middle|\, r > p\right\}\right) - 1.$$

Similarly, we obtain a safe lower bound $x_l = x_0 - \delta_l$, by finding the maximal $\delta_l \in \mathbb{Z}$ such that:

- $\delta_l \geq 0$ (it should be a *lower* bound),
- $\delta_l \leq x_0$ (lower bound does not overflow),
- $\forall x.(0 \leq x \leq \delta_l \rightarrow 2^w > a - px > b - rx \geq 0)$.

A sequence of transformations leads us to the formula

$$\delta_l = \min\left(\left\{x_0 + 1, \lceil\frac{b+1}{r}\rceil\right\} \cup \left\{\lceil\frac{a-b}{p-r}\rceil \,\middle|\, p > r\right\}\right) - 1.$$

Remark 2. At the beginning of this section, we embedded the coefficients p, q from $\mathbb{Z}/2^w\mathbb{Z}$ into $\mathbb{Q}$ by choosing the representative in the interval $[0; 2^w[$. However, whenever p or q is a large value near 2^w we may obtain better bounds by interpreting them as negative numbers, i.e., choose the representative in the interval $[-2^w; 0[$ instead. To obtain a uniform formula, we can simply plug in $p - 2^w$ and $q - 2^w$ for p and q (or just one of them), respectively, in the formulas above. In total, this gives us four different ways to estimate each bound. Since each of these computations finds a safe bound, we choose the best among them.

Remark 3 (Strict Inequalities). Finally, if we want to compute such bounds for a strict inequality $px + q <_u rx + s$, we only have to change the strictness of one inequality in our initial conditions, i.e., replace $a \pm px > b \pm rx$ by $a \pm px \geq b \pm rx$. In the final formulas, this manifests as replacing $a - b$ in the numerator by $a - b + 1$; otherwise, the results are unchanged.

5.3 Projecting Intervals to Sub-slices

Since value assignments are propagated eagerly across bit-vector slices by the e-graph component of PolySAT, in some cases, a bit-vector variable is assigned to a value that contradicts an interval on a super-slice of the variable. Such contradictions may also be caused by the e-graph, because it does not take into account intervals when merging nodes.

Let $x := y + z$ s.t. $|y| = u$ and $|z| = v$. Given the forbidden interval $x \notin [l; h[$, then $2^v y + z \notin [l; h[$. We learn intervals for y and z via the following PolySAT lemmas.

Lemma 1 (General Intervals). *In case no fixed value is known for the other sub-slice, it is possible to learn an interval as long as $[l; h[$ is big enough.*

$$len([l; h[) \geq 2^u \qquad\qquad\qquad \implies y \notin [l_y; h_y[\qquad (1)$$
$$len([l; h[) > 2^{u+v} - 2^v \qquad\qquad \implies z \notin [l_z; h_z[\qquad (2)$$

where $l_y := \lceil \frac{l}{2^v} \rceil \bmod 2^v$, $h_y := \lfloor \frac{h}{2^v} \rfloor$, $l_z := l \bmod 2^v$, and $h_z := h \bmod 2^v$.

Lemma 2 (Specific Intervals). *If the other sub-slice has a fixed value, a larger interval can be projected [17, Figure 1].*

$$z = n \wedge l_y \neq h_y \qquad\qquad\qquad\qquad \implies y \notin [l_y, h_y[\qquad (3)$$
$$z = n \wedge l_y = h_y \wedge h_y 2^v + n \in [l; h[\qquad \implies \bot \qquad\qquad (4)$$
$$y = n \wedge l_z \neq h_z \qquad\qquad\qquad\qquad \implies z \notin [l_z; h_z[\qquad (5)$$
$$y = n \wedge l_z = h_z \wedge n 2^v \in [l; h[\qquad\quad \implies \bot \qquad\qquad (6)$$

where $(\beta \in \{l, h\})$

$$\beta_y := \left\lceil \frac{(\beta - n) \bmod 2^{u+v}}{2^v} \right\rceil \bmod 2^u, \qquad \beta_z := \begin{cases} \beta \bmod 2^v & \text{if } \lfloor \frac{\beta}{2^v} \rfloor = n, \\ 0 & \text{otherwise.} \end{cases}$$

These projections are applied iteratively in PolySAT to derive intervals for arbitrary sub-slices. At each step, a choice is made between Lemmas 1–2, depending on whether a fixed value is available at the required decision level.

Example 3. We can use the above to find an interval I such that $x = 0 \mathbin{+\!\!+} y \mathbin{+\!\!+} z \wedge z[15{:}8] = 123 \wedge x \notin [300007; 0[$ implies $y \notin I$, where $|x| = 64$ and $|y| = |z| = 16$.

- First, apply (5) to obtain $y \mathbin{+\!\!+} z \notin [300007; 0[$.
- Next, with (1) we obtain $y \mathbin{+\!\!+} z[15{:}8] \notin [1253; 0[$.
- Finally, with (3) we obtain $y \notin [5; 0[$.

6 Non-linear Conflicts

Non-linear conflicts are handled in PolySAT by saturation, incremental linearization, and bit-blasting. Saturation, incremental linearization and bit-blasting are postponed until all variables are assigned values and there are no conflicts detected by propagating bounds on linear constraints.

6.1 Saturation Lemmas

Saturation lemmas propagate consequences from non-linear constraints. The consequences are considered "simpler", when they are linear or if they contain fewer variables. Saturation lemmas, given in Lemmas 3–6, are added by PolySAT if their non-linear constraints are in the assertion trail and they evaluate to false under the current assignment in Γ.

Lemma 3 (Saturation Modulo Multiplication Inequalities). *We list a number of possible saturation rules.*

$$
\begin{aligned}
px <_u qx &\implies p \neq q \\
px <_u qx &\implies \Omega^*(p,x) &&\vee\, p \leq_u q \\
px <_u qx &\implies \Omega^*(-q,x) &&\vee\, p \leq_u q \\
px <_u qx &\implies \Omega^*(q,-x) &&\vee\, p >_u q &&\vee\, p = 0 \\
px <_u qx &\implies \Omega^*(-p,-x) &&\vee\, p >_u q &&\vee\, p = 0 \\
px \leq_u qx &\implies \Omega^*(p,x) &&\vee\, p \leq_u q &&\vee\, x = 0 \\
px \leq_u qx &\implies \Omega^*(-q,x) &&\vee\, p \leq_u q &&\vee\, x = 0 &&\vee\, q = 0 \\
px \leq_u qx &\implies \Omega^*(q,-x) &&\vee\, p \geq_u q &&\vee\, x = 0 &&\vee\, p = 0 \\
px \leq_u qx &\implies \Omega^*(-p,-x) &&\vee\, p \geq_u q &&\vee\, x = 0 &&\vee\, p = 0 \\
px + s \leq_u q &\implies \Omega^*(p,x) &&\vee\, \Omega^+(px,s) \vee pr \leq_u q \vee x <_u r \\
p \leq_u x \wedge qx \leq_u r &\implies \Omega^*(q,x) &&\vee\, pq \leq_u r \\
p \leq_u x \wedge qx <_u r &\implies \Omega^*(q,x) &&\vee\, pq <_u r \\
p <_u x \wedge qx \leq_u r &\implies \Omega^*(q,x) &&\vee\, pq <_u r &&\vee\, q = 0 \\
p <_u x \wedge qx \leq_u r &\implies \Omega^*(q,x) &&\vee\, pq <_u r &&\vee\, r = 0 \\
p \leq_u qx \wedge x \leq_u r &\implies \Omega^*(q,r) &&\vee\, p \leq_u qr \\
p <_u qx \wedge x \leq_u r &\implies \Omega^*(q,r) &&\vee\, p <_u qr \\
p \leq_u qx \wedge x <_u r &\implies \Omega^*(q,r) &&\vee\, p <_u qr &&\vee\, p = 0 \\
p \leq_u qx \wedge x <_u r &\implies \Omega^*(q,r) &&\vee\, p <_u qr &&\vee\, q = 0 \\
\end{aligned}
$$

Note that these rules do not require $x \not\sqsubseteq p,q,r,s$, so they can be applied even when the degree of x is larger than 1.

Obtaining Saturation Lemmas. Since bit-vector arithmetic does not match the intuition of standard arithmetic, it can take considerable effort to come up with saturation lemmas manually. We have therefore employed some automation to discover the rules given in Lemma 3. We start with the constraint on the LHS of the rule (e.g., $px <_u qx$) and generate a set of constraints that we want to allow in the RHS. We then add the constraints for a small fixed bit-width to Z3 and employ the MARCO algorithm [22] to find the minimal unsatisfiable subsets (MUS). Each MUS corresponds to a valid lemma; however, to be useful as saturation lemmas, we filter the candidates such that the RHS is simpler in some sense. Finally, we verify manually that the lemmas generalize to arbitrary bit-widths.

Next, we can connect overflow constraints with multiplications or decompose them to linear inequalities.

Lemma 4 (Overflow Saturation).

$$
\begin{aligned}
\neg\Omega^*(p,q) \wedge q \neq 0 &\implies p \leq_u p \cdot q \\
\bar{0}p \cdot \bar{0}q \geq_u 2^w &\implies \Omega^*(p,q) \\
\Omega^*(p,q) \wedge \neg\Omega^*(r,s) &\implies p >_u r \vee q >_u s \\
\Omega^*(p,q) \wedge p \geq_u q &\implies p \geq_u \lceil\sqrt{2^w}\rceil \\
\neg\Omega^*(p,q) \wedge p \geq_u q &\implies q <_u \lfloor\sqrt{2^w}\rfloor
\end{aligned}
$$

where $\bar{0}p$ and $\bar{0}q$ stands for a zero-extension with at least one bit of p and q, respectively. Note that here $w = |p| = |q| > 1$, since for $w = 1$ multiplication overflow is impossible.

Variables can in some cases be resolved, producing constraints that are free of resolved variables.

Lemma 5 (Saturation Modulo Equalities).

$$ax + b = 0 \land cx + d = 0 \implies ad - bc = 0$$
$$ax + b = 0 \land c[x] \qquad\implies c[-b \cdot a^{-1}] \quad \text{if } a \text{ is odd}$$

where $c[x]$ may be any constraint containing x. Note that the multiplicative inverse a^{-1} of a in $\mathbb{Z}/2^w\mathbb{Z}$ exists if and only if a is odd.

Finally, let us define the *parity* of a bit-vector x as the largest number $i \in \{0, \ldots, w\}$ such that 2^i divides x. The parity of a bit-vector can be constrained by a linear inequality, where $\text{parity}(p) \geq i \iff p2^{w-i} = 0$ for $0 < i \leq w$.

Lemma 6 (Parity Saturation). *Parity inequalities can be used to constrain values of multipliers.*

$$p \cdot q = 0 \implies \text{parity}(p) + \text{parity}(q) \geq w$$
$$p \cdot q = 1 \implies \text{parity}(p) = 0$$
$$p \cdot q = q \implies \text{parity}(p - 1) + \text{parity}(q) \geq w$$
$$\text{parity}(p \cdot q) = \min(w, \text{parity}(p) + \text{parity}(q))$$

6.2   Incremental Linearization

POLYSAT includes incremental linearization rules for the cases where variables are 0, 1, −1, or powers of two. Note that our vocabulary of incremental linearization lemmas is considerably smaller than what is used for non-linear integer arithmetic [9], but it is also materially different as it operates over modular semantics of bit-vector operations. Notably, we do not include here inferences for deriving ordering constraints, such as $a > b \land c > 0 \implies ac > bc$, which holds for integers, but not for bit-vectors. Note that Lemma 3 includes ordering constraints, but only for the cases where relevant uses of multiplication do not overflow.

Lemma 7 (Incremental Linearization).

$$p = 0 \quad\implies p \cdot q = 0$$
$$p = 1 \quad\implies p \cdot q = q$$
$$p = -1 \implies p \cdot q = -q$$
$$p = 2^k \quad\implies p \cdot q = 2^k q \quad (k = 1, \ldots, w - 1)$$
$$p \cdot q = 1 \implies p = 1 \lor \Omega^*(p, q)$$
$$p \cdot q = q \implies p = 1 \lor q = 0 \lor \Omega^*(p, q)$$

6.3   Bit-Blasting Rules

As a final resort, POLYSAT admits bit-blasting. A product $x := p \cdot q$ can be equivalently represented as $\sum_i 2^i p[i] q$. The other primitive operations (bit-wise *and*, bit-wise *or*, left shift, logical and arithmetic right shift) are unfolded using blasting as follows.

Lemma 8 $(x := p \,\&\, q)$. *Bit-wise and "&" is handled using standard axioms, that fall back to bit-blasting at each index i if the basic algebraic properties hold, but x still does not evaluate to the bit-wise and of p, q.*

$$
\begin{aligned}
\top &\implies x \leq_{\mathsf{u}} p \\
p = 0 &\implies x = 0 \\
p = -1 &\implies x = q \\
p = q &\implies x = p \\
p[i] \wedge q[i] &\implies x[i] \quad \text{for each } 0 \leq i < w \\
x[i] &\implies p[i] \quad \text{for each } 0 \leq i < w
\end{aligned}
$$

Note that we do not list symmetric rules, e.g., $x \leq_{\mathsf{u}} q$.

Lemma 9 $(x := p \,|\, q)$. *Bit-wise or is handled similarly as bit-wise and.*

$$
\begin{aligned}
\top &\implies x \geq_{\mathsf{u}} p \\
p = 0 &\implies x = q \\
p = -1 &\implies x = -1 \\
p = q &\implies x = p \\
p[i] &\implies x[i] \quad \text{for each } 0 \leq i < w \\
x[i] &\implies p[i] \vee q[i] \text{ for each } 0 \leq i < w
\end{aligned}
$$

Lemma 10 $(x := p \ll q)$. *For shift operations, we split on the second argument.*

$$
\begin{aligned}
q \geq_{\mathsf{u}} w &\implies x = 0 \\
q = 0 &\implies x = p \\
q = i &\implies x = 2^i p
\end{aligned}
$$

for all constants i such that $0 < i < w$.

Lemma 11 $(x := p \gg q)$. *Logical right-shift is analogous.*

$$
\begin{aligned}
q \geq_{\mathsf{u}} w &\implies x = 0 \\
q = 0 &\implies x = p \\
q = i &\implies 2^i x \leq_{\mathsf{u}} p \leq_{\mathsf{u}} 2^i x + 2^i - 1 \wedge x <_{\mathsf{u}} 2^{w-i}
\end{aligned}
$$

for all constants i such that $0 < i < w$.

Lemma 12 $(x := p \gg_{\mathsf{a}} q)$. *The arithmetic right-shift must take into account the sign bit $p[w-1]$.*

$$
\begin{aligned}
p[w-1] \wedge q \geq_{\mathsf{u}} w &\implies x = -1 \\
\neg p[w-1] \wedge q \geq_{\mathsf{u}} w &\implies x = 0 \\
q \geq_{\mathsf{u}} w &\implies x + 1 \leq_{\mathsf{u}} 1 \\
q = 0 &\implies x = p \\
q = i &\implies 2^i x \leq_{\mathsf{u}} p \leq_{\mathsf{u}} 2^i x + 2^i - 1 \\
p[w-1] \wedge q = i &\implies x \geq_{\mathsf{u}} 2^w - 2^{w-i-1} \\
\neg p[w-1] \wedge q = i &\implies x <_{\mathsf{u}} 2^{w-i-1}
\end{aligned}
$$

for all constants i such that $0 < i < w$.

POLYSAT also performs partial bit-blasting for multiplication overflow predicates. It is based on partitioning the conditions for overflow by using the sum of most significant bits into three cases. To describe these, first let us define the shorthand $\text{msb}(p)$ for the one-based index of the most significant bit of p. For example, $\text{msb}(1) = 1, \text{msb}(2) = 2$. It can be defined indirectly using the equivalence $\text{msb}(p) \geq i \Longleftrightarrow p \geq_u 2^{i-1}$ for $1 \leq i \leq w$. The cases are

$$\text{msb}(p) + \text{msb}(q) \geq w + 2 \implies \Omega^*(p, q)$$
$$\text{msb}(p) + \text{msb}(q) \leq w \qquad \implies \neg\Omega^*(p, q)$$
$$\text{msb}(p) + \text{msb}(q) = w + 1 \implies \left(\Omega^*(p, q) \Longleftrightarrow (0p) \cdot (0q) \geq_u 2^w\right),$$

where $0p$ and $0q$ stand for the zero-extension by a single bit of p and q, respectively. In other words, when the most significant bits add up to w, multiplication overflow affects exactly one additional bit, so it suffices to extend p and q by a single bit to determine overflow.

Table 1. Number of problems solved within 60 s for several benchmark sets. The upper five solvers are based on bit-blasting, while the lower four solvers use word-level techniques.

		SMT-LIB		BV2SMV		Smart Contracts		Alive2	
		sat	unsat	sat	unsat	sat	unsat	sat	unsat
Bit-blasting	BITWUZLA [28]	17 745	27 203	32	115	1	3	39	3 954
	CVC5 [2]	16 417	25 922	31	114	0	4	39	2 722
	STP [16]	17 462	27 011	24	115	-	-	39	2 893
	YICES2 [13]	17 589	26 600	24	107	0	3	39	1 519
	Z3 [25]	16 112	25 597	29	94	0	3	39	1 514
Word-lvl	CVC5-IntBlast [36]	11 251	24 376	32	64	1	9	5	1 047
	YICES2-mcsat [17]	14 155	22 396	24	101	1	4	23	2 562
	Z3-IntBlast	10 912	24 371	28	56	1	5	30	921
	Z3-POLYSAT	7 297	20 080	28	63	0	3	0	21
	Total	46 191		192		14		12 951	

7 Experiments

We evaluated our POLYSAT prototype[1] against recent versions of several state-of-the-art SMT solvers on the following four benchmark sets: the category QF_BV

---

[1] Available at https://github.com/Z3Prover/z3/tree/poly. This paper refers to commit 16fb86b636047fd79ad5827f768b6f26d8812948. To select POLYSAT for bit-vector solving, add the following options: `sat.smt=true tactic.default_tactic=smt smt.bv.solver=1`.

from SMT-LIB [3] (release 2023, non-incremental); the BV2SMV benchmarks featuring large bit-widths [15]; 14 benchmarks from smart contract verification related to the Certora prover [1]; and a set of benchmarks from the Alive2 compiler verification project [23]. Note that the STP solver [16] does not support the logic `QF_UFBV` used by some of the Certora benchmarks.

Our experiments were performed on a TU Wien cluster, where each compute node contains two AMD Epyc 7502 processors, each of which has 32 CPU cores running at 2.5 GHz. Each compute node is equipped with 1008 GiB of physical memory that is split into eight memory nodes of 126 GiB each, with eight logical CPUs assigned to each node. We used `runexec` from the benchmarking framework BENCHEXEC [5] to assign each benchmark process to a different CPU core and its corresponding memory node. Further, we used GNU PARALLEL [32] to schedule benchmark processes in parallel.

Our results are summarized in Table 1 and indicate that POLYSAT is comparable to the other word-level approaches on the BV2SMV benchmark set, however in general, more work is needed. Concerning the Alive2 benchmarks that were solved by YICES2-mcsat but not by POLYSAT, we found that in all but three cases YICES2-mcsat did not use any interval reasoning for conflicts/propagation; rather, YICES2-mcsat relied mostly on a fallback to bit-blasting. As POLYSAT does not yet have such a fallback, this result suggests our bit-blasting rules (Sect. 6.3) alone are not enough.

Nevertheless, POLYSAT complements Z3 with word-level bit-vector reasoning. Our experimental analysis found that POLYSAT solved 135 problems that Z3 did not solve and 404 problems that Z3-IntBlast did not solve (40 of which neither Z3 nor Z3-IntBlast solved). Further combinations of complementary approaches of word-level reasoning with bit-blasting is a promising direction to explore.

8 Conclusion

We introduced POLYSAT, a general purpose word-level bit-vector solver, to overcome the scalability issue of bit-blasting over large bit-vectors. POLYSAT integrates into CDCL(T)-based SMT solving, generalizes interval-based reasoning, and performs incremental linearization of constraints. POLYSAT is implemented in the SMT solver Z3 and complements bit-vector reasoning in Z3.

Acknowledgements. We thank Mooly Sagiv and Alexander Nutz for thorough discussions on POLYSAT applications.This work was partially supported by the ERC Consolidator Grant ARTIST 101002685, the TU Wien Doctoral College SecInt, the FWF SFB project SpyCoDe F8504, the FWF ESPRIT grant 10.55776/ESP666, the WWTF Grant ForSmart 10.47379/ICT22007, and the Amazon Research Award 2023 QuAT.

Disclosure of Interests. The authors have no competing interests to declare that are relevant to the content of this article.

References

1. Albert, E., Grossman, S., Rinetzky, N., Rodríguez-Núñez, C., Rubio, A., Sagiv, M.: Taming callbacks for smart contract modularity. Proc. ACM Program. Lang. 4(OOPSLA), 1–30 (2020). https://doi.org/10.1145/3428277
2. Barbosa, H., et al.: cvc5: a versatile and industrial-strength SMT solver. In: Proceedings of TACAS, pp. 415–442 (2022). https://doi.org/10.1007/978-3-030-99524-9_24
3. Barrett, C., Fontaine, P., Tinelli, C.: The satisfiability Modulo theories library (SMT-LIB) (2016). www.SMT-LIB.org
4. Bayardo, Jr., R.J., Schrag, R.: Using CSP look-back techniques to solve real-world SAT instances. In: Proceedings of AAAI and IAAI, pp. 203–208 (1997)
5. Beyer, D., Löwe, S., Wendler, P.: Reliable benchmarking: requirements and solutions. J. Softw. Tools Technol. Transf. 21(1), 1–29 (2017)
6. Bjørner, N.S., Pichora, M.C.: Deciding fixed and non-fixed size Bit-vectors. In: Proceedings of TACAS, pp. 376–392 (1998). https://doi.org/10.1007/BFB0054184
7. Bruttomesso, R., et al.: A lazy and layered SMT($\mathcal{BV}$) solver for hard industrial verification problems. In: Proceedings of CAV. LNCS, vol. 4590, pp. 547–560. Springer (2007). https://doi.org/10.1007/978-3-540-73368-3_54
8. Bruttomesso, R., Sharygina, N.: A scalable decision procedure for fixed-width Bit-vectors. In: Proceedings of ICCAD, pp. 13–20 (2009). https://doi.org/10.1145/1687399.1687403
9. Cimatti, A., Griggio, A., Irfan, A., Roveri, M., Sebastiani, R.: Experimenting on solving nonlinear integer arithmetic with incremental linearization. In: Proceedings of SAT, pp. 383–398 (2018). https://doi.org/10.1007/978-3-319-94144-8_23
10. Cimatti, A., Griggio, A., Schaafsma, B.J., Sebastiani, R.: The MathSAT5 SMT solver. In: Proceedings of TACAS, pp. 93–107 (2013). https://doi.org/10.1007/978-3-642-36742-7_7
11. Clarke, E., Kroening, D., Lerda, F.: A tool for checking ANSI-C programs. In: Proceedings of TACAS, pp. 168–176 (2004)
12. Detlefs, D., Nelson, G., Saxe, J.B.: Simplify: a theorem prover for program checking. J. ACM 52(3), 365–473 (2005). https://doi.org/10.1145/1066100.1066102
13. Dutertre, B.: Yices 2.2. In: Proceedings of CAV, pp. 737–744 (2014). https://doi.org/10.1007/978-3-319-08867-9_49
14. Fröhlich, A., Biere, A., Wintersteiger, C.M., Hamadi, Y.: Stochastic local search for satisfiability Modulo theories. In: Proceedings of AAAI, pp. 1136–1143 (2015). http://www.aaai.org/ocs/index.php/AAAI/AAAI15/paper/view/9896
15. Fröhlich, A., Kovásznai, G., Biere, A.: Efficiently solving Bit-vector problems using model checkers. In: Proceedings of Workshop on SMT, pp. 6–15 (2013). https://fmv.jku.at/bv2smv/
16. Ganesh, V., Dill, D.L.: A decision procedure for Bit-vectors and arrays. In: Proceedings of CAV, pp. 519–531 (2007). https://doi.org/10.1007/978-3-540-73368-3_52
17. Graham-Lengrand, S., Jovanovic, D., Dutertre, B.: Solving Bitvectors with MCSAT: explanations from bits and pieces. In: Proceedings of IJCAR, pp. 103–121 (2020). https://doi.org/10.1007/978-3-030-51074-9_7
18. Hadarean, L., Bansal, K., Jovanovic, D., Barrett, C.W., Tinelli, C.: A tale of two solvers: eager and lazy approaches to bit-vectors. In: Procrrdings of CAV. LNCS, vol. 8559, pp. 680–695. Springer (2014). https://doi.org/10.1007/978-3-319-08867-9_45

19. John, A.K., Chakraborty, S.: A layered algorithm for quantifier elimination from linear modular constraints. Formal Methods Syst. Des. **49**(3), 272–323 (2016). https://doi.org/10.1007/s10703-016-0260-9
20. Kovásznai, G., Fröhlich, A., Biere, A.: Complexity of fixed-size bit-vector logics. Theory Comput. Syst. **59**(2), 323–376 (2016). https://doi.org/10.1007/s00224-015-9653-1
21. Kroening, D., Strichman, O.: Decision Procedures - An Algorithmic Point of View. Springer (2008). https://doi.org/10.1007/978-3-540-74105-3
22. Liffiton, M.H., Previti, A., Malik, A., Marques-Silva, J.: Fast, flexible MUS enumeration. Constraints An. Int. J. **21**(2), 223–250 (2016). https://doi.org/10.1007/S10601-015-9183-0
23. Lopes, N.P., Lee, J., Hur, C.K., Liu, Z., Regehr, J.: Alive2: bounded translation validation for LLVM. In: Proceedings of PLDI, pp. 65–79 (2021). https://doi.org/10.1145/3453483.3454030
24. Möller, M.O., Rueß, H.: Solving bit-vector equations. In: Proceedings of FMCAD, pp. 36–48 (1998). https://doi.org/10.1007/3-540-49519-3_4
25. de Moura, L.M., Bjørner, N.S.: Z3: an efficient SMT solver. In: Proceedings of TACAS, pp. 337–340 (2008). https://doi.org/10.1007/978-3-540-78800-3_24
26. de Moura, L.M., Jovanovic, D.: A model-constructing satisfiability calculus. In: International Conference on Verification, Model Checking, and Abstract Interpretation (VMCAI). LNCS, vol. 7737, pp. 1–12. Springer (2013). https://doi.org/10.1007/978-3-642-35873-9_1
27. Niemetz, A., Preiner, M.: Ternary propagation-based local search for more bit-precise reasoning. In: Proceedings of FMCAD, pp. 214–224 (2020). https://doi.org/10.34727/2020/isbn.978-3-85448-042-6_29
28. Niemetz, A., Preiner, M.: Bitwuzla. In: Proceedings of CAV, pp. 3–17 (2023). https://doi.org/10.1007/978-3-031-37703-7_1
29. Niemetz, A., Preiner, M., Biere, A.: Propagation based local search for bit-precise reasoning. Formal Methods Syst. Design **51**(3), 608–636 (2017). https://doi.org/10.1007/s10703-017-0295-6
30. Niemetz, A., Preiner, M., Zohar, Y.: Scalable bit-blasting with abstractions. In: Proceedings of CAV, pp. 178–200 (2024). https://doi.org/10.1007/978-3-031-65627-9_9
31. Silva, J., Sakallah, K.A.: GRASP: a search algorithm for propositional satisfiability. IEEE Trans. Comput. **48**(5), 506–521 (1999). https://doi.org/10.1109/12.769433
32. Tange, O.: GNU Parallel 20240122 ('Frederik X'), GNU Parallel is a general parallelizer to run multiple serial command line programs in parallel without changing them (2024). https://doi.org/10.5281/zenodo.10558745
33. Wang, W., Søndergaard, H., Stuckey, P.J.: Wombit: a portfolio bitvector solver using word-level propagation. J. Autom. Reason. **63**(3), 723–762 (2019). https://doi.org/10.1007/s10817-018-9493-1
34. Willsey, M., Nandi, C., Wang, Y.R., Flatt, O., Tatlock, Z., Panchekha, P.: egg: fast and extensible equality saturation. Proc. ACM Program. Lang. **5**(POPL), 1–29 (2021). https://doi.org/10.1145/3434304
35. Zeljic, A., Wintersteiger, C.M., Rümmer, P.: Deciding Bit-Vector Formulas with mcSAT. In: Proceedings of SAT, pp. 249–266 (2016). https://doi.org/10.1007/978-3-319-40970-2_16
36. Zohar, Y., et al.: Bit-precise reasoning via Int-blasting. In: Proceedings of VMCAI, pp. 496–518 (2022). https://doi.org/10.1007/978-3-030-94583-1_24

Proof-Producing Symbolic Execution
for P4

Didrik Lundberg[1,2]($\boxtimes$) (ORCID), Roberto Guanciale[1,3] (ORCID), and Mads Dam[1] (ORCID)

[1] KTH Royal Institute of Technology, Lindstedtsvägen 5, 100 44 Stockholm, Sweden
{didrikl,robertog,mfd}@kth.se
[2] Saab AB, Nettovägen 6, 175 41 Järfälla, Sweden
[3] Digital Futures, Osquars Backe 5, 100 44 Stockholm, Sweden

Abstract. We introduce a proof-producing symbolic execution tool for formal verification of P4 programs. The tool has been implemented using the interactive theorem prover HOL4 and results are proved sound with respect to the HOL4P4 formalisation of the P4 language. Most notably, this is a general tool for proving functional correctness that can be applied to entire real-world P4 programs.

Keywords: Theorem Proving · Formal Verification · Domain-Specific Languages

1 Introduction

P4 is the most popular domain-specific language for the data planes of programmable network elements, the hardware which the software-defined networking (SDN) paradigm is built on. A software-defined network element separates packet processing functionality into the control plane (which updates tables with network topology and routing information) and the data plane (which performs the actual bit-by-bit processing of packets). The interface between these two planes is kept minimal. There exists a diverse range of targets for P4 from terabit-bandwidth switches to network interface controllers and the Linux kernel [9,23].

Network elements that govern communication in critical systems must undergo strict high-assurance certification. For the highest levels of certification, formal verification is required - and for this, using an interactive theorem prover (ITP) is ideal. The simplicity of P4 (absence of pointers, unbounded loops and recursion) means that exhaustive formal reasoning needs to perform less computation, rendering heavy-duty formal methods feasible for large programs.

The contributions[1] presented in this paper are:

---

[1] The code for the tool presented in this paper can be found in the Github repository at https://github.com/kth-step/HOL4P4 and the version as of writing this paper at the tag VSTTE2024. The parts related to symbolic execution are found in the `hol/symb_exec` directory.

© The Author(s), under exclusive license to Springer Nature Switzerland AG 2025
J. Protzenko and A. Raad (Eds.): VSTTE 2024, LNCS 15525, pp. 70–83, 2025.
https://doi.org/10.1007/978-3-031-86695-1_5

1. A concurrent, language-agnostic HOL4 symbolic execution framework (Sect. 4).
2. A formal verification tool for P4 programs that only requires minimal annotation (Sect. 5), including automated overapproximation methods for interaction with external functions and data (Sect. 5.2), and usage of multiple small-step semantics of different scope and granularity for increased efficiency (Sect. 5.3).
3. Performance evaluation for a case study for the above (Sect. 7).

2 Background and Related Work

2.1 The P4 Language

P4 programs are structured as a pipeline consisting of programmable blocks. These programmable blocks are either parser blocks or control blocks. Parser blocks are similar to finite state machines: they consist of parser states which typically extract the bits of the input packet into P4 headers (similar to C structs), with unstructured jumps between them. Control blocks consist of (possibly branching) sequences of look-ups in tables configured by the control plane, without loops. When verifying a P4 program, the content of some tables may be known, while the content of others may be unknown.

Throughout P4 programs, external functions and objects (typically implemented by the architecture in an FPGA or directly in ASICs) provide more complex functionality such as hashing and checksum computation.

To illustrate significant language features, Figs. 1 and 2 contain snippets of a simplified version of the VSS example found in the P4 Specification [22]. The program parses an Ethernet and an IPv4 header of an input packet, validates the IPv4 checksum, then sets the output port based on the IPv4 destination address. Figure 1 shows the parser block `TopParser` with the initial parser state `start`. The `extract` method fills its struct arguments with bits from the raw input packet `b`. The fields of the structs can then be accessed, as seen on line 8 of Fig. 1. The `select` expression matches the argument - here, the `etherType` field of `p.ethernet` - to value sets in a list (here the singleton set {0x8000} and the set of all 16-bit values), and chooses the corresponding next parser state for the transition statement based on this match.

The external `Checksum16` object `ck` in Fig. 1 can compute checksums from IPv4 headers. External objects and functions do not have implementations written in P4: they are provided by the target platform.

The `verify` statement checks that the predicate given as first argument holds. If not, the parser block will transition to the `reject` state and set `parseError` outside the programmable blocks to `verify`'s second argument.

The parser block is finished upon transitioning to the `accept` or `reject` state, after which the out-directed block parameter `p` is copied out, to be used later. Then, execution of the control block `TopPipe` shown in Fig. 2 commences: `p` and `parseError` are copied in, and the content of the apply block between lines 18 and 24 is executed.

```
1 parser TopParser(packet_in b,
2                 out Parsed_packet p) {
3   Checksum16() ck;
4
5   state start {
6     b.extract(p.ethernet);
7     transition
8     select(p.ethernet.etherType) {
9       0x0800: parse_ipv4;
10      _: reject;
11    }
12  }
13
14  state parse_ipv4 {
15    b.extract(p.ip);
16    ck.clear();
17    ck.update(p.ip);
18    verify(ck.get() == 16w0,
19           error.IPv4ChecksumError);
20    transition accept;
21  }
22 }
```

```
1 control TopPipe(inout Parsed_packet p,
2                 in error parseError,
3                 out OutControl outCtrl) {
4   action Drop_action() {
5     outCtrl.outputPort = DROP_PORT;
6   }
7
8   action Set_oport(PortId port) {
9     outCtrl.outputPort = port;
10  }
11
12  table ipv4_match {
13    key = {p.ip.dstAddr: lpm;}
14    actions = {Drop_action;
15               Set_oport;}
16  }
17
18  apply {
19    if (parseError == error.NoError) {
20      ipv4_match.apply();
21    } else {
22      Drop_action();
23    }
24  }
25 }
```

Fig. 1. Parser block snippet   **Fig. 2.** Control block snippet.

The table application `ipv4_match.apply()` on line 20 looks up the value in the key of `ipv4_match` (`p.ip.dstAddr`) in a table stored in the control plane: note that the entries of the table are left unspecified by the P4 program. `lpm` signifies a longest-prefix match, and the outcome of this match is the invocation of either of the `actions`: `Drop_action` or `Set_nhop`, with arguments provided by the control plane.

2.2 Related Work

Symbolic execution [13] summarises many execution traces into one, at the expense of having to fork execution into multiple paths upon encountering branches in the control flow. While the classic notion of symbolic execution allows omitting traces from analysis (i.e. underapproximation), this trace exclusion does not allow for proving safety properties. Conversely, safety properties can be proved using trace overapproximation. As such, the flavour of symbolic execution used in this work is in a sense "trace-complete" or "overapproximating".

At least since the 90 s [21], it has been known that theorem provers offer a shortcut to implementing something akin to symbolic execution by evaluating terms with native free variables in place of concrete values. In the literature, this shallow embedding of symbolic execution is also known as *symbolic simulation* or *symbolic evaluation*. This technique implements symbolic branching in the metalanguage, which does not yield a formal definition for which to prove e.g. termination (of the symbolic execution itself). However, the absence of a termination proof has no adverse effect on the soundness of the analysis.

Symbolic Execution Using HOL4. Holfoot [24,25] is a tool that uses shallowly embedded symbolic execution and an abstract separation logic to verify functional correctness of programs in the Smallfoot language. Note that using separation logic for P4 is unnecessary, since the language does not involve pointer arithmetic.

Collavizza and Gordon [4] have used shallowly embedded symbolic execution to formally verify properties of Java programs, using an approach that depends in part on unverified reasoning.

Campbell and Stark [3], and more recently Kanabar et al. [11], use shallowly embedded symbolic execution based on the `step` library of Anthony Fox [6] for test generation, compiler verification and cross-validation of ISA models.

Lindner [14] et al. describe a deeply embedded symbolic execution for the unstructured BIR language used for binary analysis. The deeply-embedded approach allows to prove a formal metatheory about the symbolic execution itself.

In comparison to the above, our work is unique through the usage of multiple small-step semantics of different scope and granularity to improve efficiency of symbolic evaluation, overapproximation techniques and the contribution of a language-agnostic symbolic execution framework.

There exists a plethora of tools for other ITPs that use symbolic execution-based techniques for formal verification [8,12,16,19]: to the authors' knowledge no comprehensive review comparing symbolic execution in different ITPs exists. The authors could also not identify any other ITP-based work that combines multiple symbolic semantic styles and uses automated overapproximation.

P4 Verification. P4Cub [18] is an intermediate representation for P4 verification with both big-step and small-step semantics formalised in Coq that has been used for a non-proof-producing program verifier. Wang et al. introduce Verifiable P4 [26], a verification system implemented in Coq that uses semi-automatic symbolic execution techniques together with reasoning in program logic to prove correctness of P4 control blocks. In contrast, the symbolic execution presented in this paper is fully automatic and covers the entire P4 pipeline. Leapfrog [5] is an equivalence checker for P4 parsers implemented in Coq.

Vera [20] and P4pktgen [17] both use underapproximating symbolic execution to find bugs in P4 programs. ASSERT-P4 [7] and p4v [15] are other non-proof-producing verification tools for P4.

3   HOL4P4 Semantics

To implement the symbolic execution approach of this paper in an ITP, an executable semantics is needed: here, "executable" means that reduction results can be computed directly using standard evaluation facilities of the ITP. This executable semantics is a deeply embedded function $small(E, \rho, n)$ that computes the result of n reductions (i.e. the transitive closure of n small-step reductions) of the initial state ρ in the static environment E according to the semantics' reduction rules. This work is built on the HOL4P4 semantics of Alshnakat et al.

[1]², presented in brief below, simplified for the sake of presentation. For brevity, this executable semantics will be referred to simply as the "small-step semantics" in the rest of the paper.

The semantics consists of four layers: architecture, frame, statement, and expression. The architecture layer connects the programmable blocks and governs input and output. The frame layer ensures that the frame resulting from the most recently called function is passed along to the statement semantics, and handles function return.

All architecture-level reductions are made in the presence of a static environment E, which contains the program and models of external functions. The architecture-level state $\rho = (\overline{io}, \alpha, i, \gamma_G, \overline{\Phi}, t)$ consists of lists of incoming and outgoing packets $\overline{io}$, an external state (of the runtime) α, the current block index i, a global store γ_G, a frame stack $\overline{\Phi}$ and a status t. The status is used for signaling function return and parser block transition from the statement-level to the frame- and architecture-level semantics. Each frame in $\overline{\Phi}$ corresponds to a called function, with the top frame popped upon function return: functions are restricted to manipulating their own frames. A frame $\Phi = s \, {}^{f}_{\gamma}$ consists of the associated function's name f, the statement currently being reduced s, and a variable store γ holding the values of local variables.

The frame layer reduces $(\alpha, \gamma_G, \overline{\Phi}, t)$ to tuples of the same type, with table and function signatures from E in the local context. The statement layer has the same signature as the frame layer, but with a single frame Φ instead. The expression layer reduces expressions e to expressions (and a new frame in case of function call), with the function signatures from E and the current scopes (γ and γ_G) in the local context.

Figure 3 showcases the statement-level semantic rule for table application using a fully reduced key $v_1,...,v_n$ (a separate rule reduces the key using the expression-level semantics). As an example, consider line 20 of Fig. 2. Here, the key consists of a single element: the value of `p.ip.dstAddr`. Using the static table information stored in T (the match kind `lpm`), the key will be matched to entries of `match_ipv4` stored in α. The match result is an action f' with arguments $v'_1,...,v'_m$, and the **apply** statement reduces to a call to this action. The status is retained as **run**, signifying regular execution.

APPLY
$$\frac{T\,(tbl, v_1,...,v_n, \alpha) = (f',\, v'_1,...,v'_m)}{T\,F \vdash (\alpha, \gamma_G, [\textbf{apply } tbl\ v_1,...,v_n] \, {}^{f}_{\gamma}, \textbf{run}) \to (\alpha, \gamma_G, [\textbf{null} := f'(v'_1,...,v'_m)] \, {}^{f}_{\gamma}, \textbf{run})}$$

Fig. 3. Semantic rule for table application

The statements consist of the standard assignment, block, conditional and return and the P4-specific extern statement ■, **transition** and **apply**.

---

² A small extension to HOL4P4 is used, which adds value set types used for matching in **select** expressions.

The extern statement ■ can implement any behaviour that modifies α and the local γ. Reduction of ■ uses the function name f of the current frame, and looks up the implementation in the static environment: $E(f) = ext$, then uses it to update α and γ: $ext(\alpha, \gamma_G, \gamma) = (\alpha', \gamma', t')$, where t' is the resulting status.

transition is similar to a jump, with possible targets being different parser states in the same programmable block.

Finally, **apply** matches a list of expressions $\overline{e}$ against a table tbl stored in α: $match(\overline{e}, tbl, \alpha) = a(\overline{arg})$. Then, **apply** is reduced to a call to the result $a(\overline{arg})$. Notably, ■ and **apply** are the only statements that interact with α.

The expressions consist of standard arithmetic and Boolean operators together with function calls (generating new frames when reduced) and the **select** expression, which is typically found together with the **transition** statement. **select** can be thought of as matching against membership in value sets. Values are modeled with bit-level granularity, and we represent e.g. a bit-string of width 4 as $b_1 b_2 b_3 b_4$, with $b_1 \ldots b_4$ being the individual bits.

4 Symbolic Execution Framework

4.1 Shallow Symbolic Execution

The goal of the symbolic execution approach presented here is to provide a generic tool that requires only an executable small-step semantics and minimal proof additions to enable symbolic execution, while still allowing for incremental performance improvements.

The basic idea for re-using an executable semantics for symbolic execution is as follows:

1. To model symbolic values, use HOL4 native free variables in place of concrete values.
2. Prevent state explosion by restricting evaluation of arithmetic dependent on free variables when reducing expressions to values: for example, not unfolding the definition of (primitive) addition of bitstrings in $b_1 b_2 b_3 + 010$, where b_1, b_2 and b_3 are HOL4 free variables of bit type. The result can then get assigned to a variable as-is.
3. Fork the symbolic execution whenever a branch is dependent on a HOL4 free variable, maintaining a list of n-step theorems with path conditions:

$$P \implies small(\rho, n) = \rho'$$

stating that given the path condition P, n small-step execution steps from ρ results in ρ'. Note that P and ρ can share HOL4 free variables. $small$ is a partial function that is undefined when a run-time error occurs, which can be implemented using an option type.

With this approach, it is not necessary to modify the executable semantics in any way. The maintenance of separate n-step theorems for separate paths means that the semantics does not have to formalise the notion of paths or path conditions.

Around 200 additional lines of HOL4 proof scripts are needed for a minimal implementation of HOL4P4 symbolic execution. Note that the symbolic execution can not in general produce a strongest postcondition, since it allows overapproximation. If no overapproximation was used, the strongest predicate obeyed by the final state of every path can be informally thought of as the strongest postcondition.

4.2   N-Chotomy Theorems

To prove no execution traces are dropped by the symbolic execution, it is necessary to prove an *n-chotomy theorem* every time the symbolic execution is forked. This theorem exhaustively enumerates as disjuncts all possible outcomes that might result from values of the free variables in the construct that the semantics branches on. For example, the n-chotomy theorem of the `select` expression on line 8 of Fig. 1 would state that $b_1 \dots b_{16} \in \{0x8000\} \lor b_1 \dots b_{16} \notin \{0x8000\}$, where $b_1 \dots b_{16}$ is the result of reducing `p.ethernet.etherType`.

After the n-chotomy theorem has been proved, some disjuncts may be immediately ruled out (pruned) using the path condition. Then, the symbolic execution is forked, with each new path condition gaining (by conjunction) one disjunct from the n-chotomy theorem. The n-chotomy theorems themselves are stored in a tree structure that keeps track of which paths resulted from which choices: every non-leaf node holds an n-chotomy theorem and every leaf holds a unique identifier that pairs it with a path (n-step theorem). The n-chotomy tree is used later when proving properties about the result of the symbolic execution.

4.3   Abstract Symbolic Execution Algorithm

Part of the symbolic execution machinery is language-agnostic and has therefore been written as an abstract framework that can be instantiated to perform symbolic execution of other languages. The language parameters are the following functions:

1. `regular_step`: takes the current n-step theorem and performs m regular execution steps starting from the current state, then composes the result with the previous, yielding an $n + m$-step theorem. The simplest possible implementation would just rely on direct evaluation of the executable semantics used, doable in less than 10 LoC in HOL4.
2. `should_branch`: looks at the current n-step theorem and decides whether to fork the symbolic execution or not. If yes, it returns an n-chotomy theorem and a list of forked n-step theorems, to whose path conditions the cases of the n-chotomy theorem have been added.
3. `is_finished`: looks at the current n-step theorem and decides whether execution on that path has finished or not.

The final output of the symbolic execution algorithm is a list of n-step theorems (as described in Sect. 4) and a tree with n-chotomy theorems (as described in Sect. 5.2). Provided the implementations of `regular_step`, `should_branch` and `is_finished` are thread-safe, the abstract symbolic execution framework is capable of running them concurrently. Concurrency is achieved via a simple mutex-based job scheduler that synchronizes the common datastructure holding the n-chotomy tree and n-step theorems.

4.4   Coarse-Grained Semantics

The semantics of a language may have notions of locality that permit simplified reductions inside different locales. Perhaps the most obvious one is the locale of functions: restricting the semantics to reductions inside individual functions can strip the semantics of much complexity. Another optimization can be done for semantics with multiple layers, where collapsing multiple steps into one can effectively "cache" computations from layers above. The HOL4P4 case of this optimization is shown in Fig. 4. This paper uses "coarse-grained semantics" to refer to the type of semantics with restrictions and optimizations described by the above paragraph relative to the base small-step semantics.

To use a coarse-grained together with a fine-grained small-step semantics, it is necessary to compose their executions: this can be done via the usual composition theorems for small-step execution so long as a soundness theorem, like Proposition 1, is proved. This is stated relative to some *update* and *proj*: the function *proj* extracts information from ρ to construct a coarse-grained state s, and *update* takes a resulting coarse-grained state and modifies ρ accordingly.

Proposition 1 (Soundness of Coarse-Grained Semantics). *If* $proj(\rho) = s$, $coarse(s) = (s', n)$ *and* $update(\rho, s') = \rho'$, *then* $small(\rho, n) = \rho'$.

5   HOL4P4 Symbolic Execution

5.1   Regular HOL4P4 Execution Steps

"Regular" steps are steps where no overapproximation or fork of the symbolic execution occurs. However, regular steps may still involve operations using symbolic variables. The regular execution step implementation is based on the call-by-value reduction engine `CBV_CONV` [2] with a custom `compset` of rewrites and conversions. In addition to this, rewriting using the path condition is also performed as needed: typically this involves restricting evaluation of some functions (using `RESTR_CBV_CONV`), rewriting, and then resuming evaluation without this restriction. Some functions involving arithmetic are never evaluated in the main loop to prevent state explosion - instead, they are selectively extracted and evaluated separately. At the end, the result of evaluating one step from the current final state is composed with the existing n-step theorem, forming an $n + 1$-step theorem.

The main issue with this approach is the large size of the theorems involved. We have solved this in part by introducing definitions for the (very large) static environment E and its components, which are unfolded and folded back as needed. For parts of the mutable state that may contain HOL4 variables, this is more difficult, but is in part solved by a type of approximation described in Sect. 5.2. Note that in practice, the HOL4P4 symbolic execution will always terminate using repeated regular steps: the control blocks are loop-free, and realistic P4 programs either hard-code bounds on variable-length headers and extension headers, or limit their size by a preceding field determining length.

5.2   HOL4P4 N-Chotomy Theorems

Other than the conditional statement, the two other branching HOL4P4 language constructs are **select** expressions (in **transition** statements) and **apply** statements. **select** expressions match a value v to value sets $V_1, \ldots, V_n$ in a list ranked from 1 to n, with the outcomes being parser state names $st_1, \ldots, st_n$. In that case, the n-chotomy theorem would be

$$v \in V_1 \lor (v \in V_2 \land v \notin V_1) \lor \ldots \lor (v \in V_n \land v \notin V_{n-1} \cup \ldots \cup v \notin V_1)$$

with every outcome ruling out the outcomes ranked above it. Note that the value v can be a complex HOL4 term involving multiple free variables.

The **apply** case exposes some quirks of P4 and the networking setting, due to the complex match kinds and reading external table content (key-value pairs) from the control plane. For tables with known content, the resulting n-chotomy theorem looks rather similar to that for **select**.

The case when table entries are not known at verification time (for example, the table `ipv4_match` in Fig. 2) is more interesting. Since in P4, a table tbl must list all possible actions $a_1 \ldots a_n$ that can result from a match, the n-chotomy can be stated in terms of the resulting action. Such an n-chotomy theorem can only be stated assuming the entries of tbl in α are well-formed in this respect:

$$\text{well-formed}(tbl, \alpha) \Rightarrow$$
$$(\exists b_1 \ldots b_{m1}. \ \text{match}(v, tbl, \alpha) = a_1(b_0 \ldots b_{m1})) \lor \ldots$$
$$\lor (\exists b_1 \ldots b_{mn}. \ \text{match}(v, tbl, \alpha) = a_n(b_0 \ldots b_{mn}))$$

The arguments to the resulting actions have been restricted to single bitstrings of length m for the sake of presentation. Typically, the well-formedness assumptions are inserted into the initial path condition: this is justified by the P4 Specification stating the control-plane runtime is responsible for only inserting valid entries into tables. Assumptions on the values of arguments in the match result can also be inserted into the initial path condition. This is used when one has partial information of the table content: for example, that a match result will occur for all IP addresses in the local network.

Although the concrete semantics of extern objects can be modeled from their written descriptions, we often choose to overapproximate the outcome of e.g. checksum computations by using fresh HOL4 variables for the individual bits of their result. This is done by providing a list of the externs to potentially be approximated. Then it is decided whether to approximate or not based on the

γ of the top frame, and theorems are proved that overapproximate the effect of the extern (some sub-function of the extern implementation) for that γ, using existentially quantified HOL4 variables. This approximation theorem is then used like a 1-chotomy theorem by the rest of the framework.

5.3   HOL4P4 Coarse-Grained Semantics

For the HOL4P4 small-step semantics, many design choices were made that make it more suitable for a formal metatheory, but less efficient for computation. The most severe issue is that every single execution step must traverse every level from top (architecture) to bottom: first, an architectural reduction is chosen, then a frame reduction, then a statement and expression-level reduction, every layer forwarding appropriate information to the next. A more efficient approach that can be implemented as a coarse-grained executable semantics is to keep reducing on a lower layer (for example, the expression layer) until the expression is fully reduced, similar to a reduction in big-step semantics, and only then return to the layer above. This is illustrated in Fig. 4.

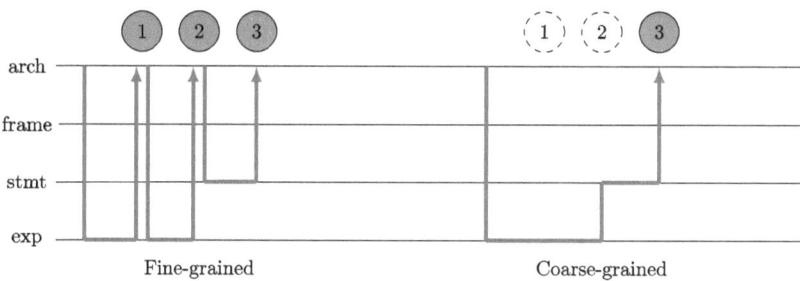

Fig. 4. Reductions on semantic layers: fine-grained vs. coarse-grained

Additionally, if the coarse-grained semantics is limited to a simple fragment of the HOL4P4 syntax (i.e., no ■, no **apply**, no function call and no **return**), it is possible to simplify the reductions greatly: the external state α can be disregarded since it is only interacted with by ■ and **apply**. The static environment E is not needed, since on the statement level it is only used for function call and **apply**. Since no function return is allowed, the status and all frames except the topmost can also be disregarded. This partiality is implemented by having the coarse-grained semantics halt once a disallowed statement is about to be reduced and return the current statement, allowing for the small-step semantics to continue from the resulting state. In practice, it is preferable to use multiple coarse-grained semantics that first treat a more complex statement using the necessary elements of ρ and E, then continue using the above minimal coarse-grained semantics.

6   Proving Contracts for HOL4P4

One use case of the symbolic execution result is to prove contracts, as defined in Definition 1: flexible enough to accommodate any functional correctness property. Note that the symbolic execution result is independent of this notion of contracts and can be used for other ends, e.g. for proving simulation theorems or in interactive proofs.

Definition 1 (Contract). *The contract* $\{P\} \, E \, \{Q\}$ *holds iff for the precondition* P, *static environment* E *and postcondition* Q

$$\forall \rho. \, P(\rho) \Rightarrow \exists n > 0. \, \exists \rho'. \, \mathrm{small}(E, \rho, n) = \rho' \wedge Q(\rho') \, .$$

Note that ρ and ρ' contain not only variable maps, but also the program currently being reduced. To avoid spurious proofs where Q only holds for some intermediate states, Q can include a finish condition (e.g. "last block was just reduced, no more input packets pending"). Also, since HOL4 functions are deterministic ρ' can be existentially quantified.

Contracts are obtained by proving that the postcondition holds for every final state of the n-step theorems resulting from the symbolic execution, after which all resulting contracts are unified to one by using the n-chotomy theorems. Should the postcondition not be provable for some path, this will be printed, providing a possible counterexample. The contract derivation procedure is fully automatic. Note that the overapproximation described in Sect. 5.2 allows proving a valid contract as long as it does not introduce new paths and if any free variables introduced does not affect the postcondition.

If the end goal is not to prove a contract with a provided postcondition, another approach could be to instead prove the postcondition of the symbolic execution: $Q(\rho) = (P_1(\rho) \Rightarrow \rho = \rho_1) \wedge \ldots \wedge (P_n(\rho) \Rightarrow \rho = \rho_n)$, where n is the number of paths. This could then also be used to prove the contract.

7   Evaluation

As a small case study, the tool has been applied to the P4 implementation of IPsec tunneling by Hauser et al. [10].[3]

The overapproximation techniques have been implemented for externs from the V1Model architecture, allowing to abstract from large structures and computations which would otherwise make verification infeasible. During development, we have also constructed a small validation suite of P4 programs with pre- and postconditions. Some performance numbers are shown in Table 1: lines of code, total verification time, average reduction times for fine-grained and coarse-grained, and the number of paths at the end. The coarse-grained average reduction time is obtained by dividing the sum of all coarse-grained reduction

---

[3] See `hol/symb_exec/basicScript.sml`: the contract establishes the postcondition `postcond` given the precondition `path_cond`.

times with the corresponding number of fine-grained reductions. To get an idea of how the tool scales, the IPsec example (`basic.p4`) is compared to one of the validation tests (`table-unknown.p4`), an order of magnitude smaller in size. The experiments were ran on a laptop with an Intel i7-8550U CPU.

Table 1. Performance measurements

Program	LoC	Total Time	Avg. Red. Time (fine-grained)	Avg. Red. Time (coarse-grained)	Paths
`basic.p4`	396	30 m	250 ms	120 ms	82
`table-unknown.p4`	78	34 s	80 ms	30 ms	12

The generic symbolic execution framework[4] is 500 LoC and the P4-specific part 7500 LoC, of which 5000 for the coarse-grained semantics and its soundness proof. To validate the claim that the symbolic execution framework is language-agnostic, it was instantiated for a simple imperative language with while loops, which took about an hour of work and required 300 LoC.

8   Conclusions

We have presented a theorem-grade symbolic execution tool for P4 that is able to deal with quirks of the networking domain, by using overapproximation for external implementations and unknown table configurations.

We show how, in the ITP setting, symbolic execution can be obtained easily from the executable small-step semantics of a real language. Furthermore, a significant part of the symbolic execution machinery is generic and can be re-used for executable models of other languages. Also, we show how the performance of this style of symbolic execution can be increased by pairing it with a coarse-grained semantics.

For future work, the construction of a benchmark suite of P4 programs with functional correctness properties would be helpful when comparing the performance of different verification tools.

Acknowledgments. This work was in part financially supported by Digital Futures, and in part by the SEMLA project financed by Vinnova (Sweden's Innovation Agency). We would also like to thank the reviewers for their valuable feedback.

References

1. Alshnakat, A., Lundberg, D., Guanciale, R., Dam, M.: HOL4P4: mechanized small-step semantics for P4. Proc. ACM Program. Lang. **8**(OOPSLA1), 223–249 (2024). https://doi.org/10.1145/3649819

---

[4] The framework consists of `hol/symb_exec/symb_execScript.sml` and `hol/symb_exec/symb_execLib.sml`.

2. Barras, B.: Programming and computing in HOL. In: International Conference on Theorem Proving in Higher Order Logics, pp. 17–37. Springer (2000). https://doi.org/10.1007/3-540-44659-1_2

3. Campbell, B., Stark, I.: Extracting behaviour from an executable instruction set model. In: 2016 Formal Methods in Computer-Aided Design (FMCAD), pp. 33–40 (2016). https://doi.org/10.1109/FMCAD.2016.7886658

4. Collavizza, H., Gordon, M.: Integration of theorem-proving and constraint programming for software verification. Ph. D. thesis, Laboratoire I3S (2009)

5. Doenges, R., Kappé, T., Sarracino, J., Foster, N., Morrisett, G.: Leapfrog: certified equivalence for protocol parsers. In: Proceedings of the 43rd ACM SIGPLAN International Conference on Programming Language Design and Implementation, pp. 950–965. PLDI 2022 (2022). https://doi.org/10.1145/3519939.3523715

6. Fox, A.: Improved tool support for machine-code decompilation in HOL4. In: 6th International Conference on Interactive Theorem Proving (ITP 2015), pp. 187–202 (2015). https://doi.org/10.1007/978-3-319-22102-1_12

7. Freire, L., Neves, M., Leal, L., Levchenko, K., Schaeffer-Filho, A., Barcellos, M.: Uncovering bugs in P4 programs with assertion-based verification. In: SOSR '18, Proceedings of the Symposium on SDN Research (2018). https://doi.org/10.1145/3185467.3185499

8. Gourdin, L., Bonneau, B., Boulmé, S., Monniaux, D., Bérard, A.: Formally verifying optimizations with block simulations. Proc. ACM Program. Lang. **7**(OOPSLA2), 59–88 (2023). https://doi.org/10.1145/3622799

9. Hadi Salim, J., et al.: Introducing P4TC-a P4 implementation on Linux kernel using traffic control. In: Proceedings of the 6th on European P4 Workshop, pp. 25–32 (2023). https://doi.org/10.1145/3630047.3630193

10. Hauser, F., Häberle, M., Schmidt, M., Menth, M.: P4-IPsec: site-to-site and host-to-site VPN with IPsec in P4-based SDN. IEEE Access **8**, 139567–139586 (2020). https://doi.org/10.1109/ACCESS.2020.3012738

11. Kanabar, H., Fox, A.C., Myreen, M.O.: Taming an authoritative Armv8 ISA specification: L3 validation and CakeML compiler verification. In: 13th International Conference on Interactive Theorem Proving (ITP 2022). Schloss-Dagstuhl-Leibniz Zentrum für Informatik (2022). https://doi.org/10.4230/LIPIcs.ITP.2022.20

12. Keller, C.: Tactic program-based testing and bounded verification in Isabelle/HOL. In: Tests and Proofs: 12th International Conference, TAP 2018, Held as Part of STAF 2018, Toulouse, France, June 27–29, 2018, Proceedings 12, pp. 103–119. Springer (2018). https://doi.org/10.1007/978-3-319-92994-1_6

13. King, J.C.: Symbolic execution and program testing. Commun. ACM **19**(7), 385–394 (1976). https://doi.org/10.1145/360248.360252

14. Lindner, A., Guanciale, R., Dam, M.: Proof-producing symbolic execution for binary code verification. arXiv preprint arXiv:2304.08848 (2023)

15. Liu, J., et al.: p4v: practical verification for programmable data planes. In: SIGCOMM '18, Proceedings of the 2018 Conference of the ACM Special Interest Group on Data Communication, pp. 490–503 (2018). https://doi.org/10.1145/3230543.3230582

16. Matthews, J., Moore, J.S., Ray, S., Vroon, D.: Verification condition generation via theorem proving. In: Logic for Programming, Artificial Intelligence, and Reasoning: 13th International Conference, LPAR 2006, Phnom Penh, Cambodia, November 13–17, 2006. Proceedings 13, pp. 362–376. Springer (2006). https://doi.org/10.1007/11916277_25

17. Nötzli, A., Khan, J., Fingerhut, A., Barrett, C., Athanas, P.: P4pktgen: automated test case generation for p4 programs. In: Proceedings of the Symposium on SDN Research, pp. 1–7 (2018). https://doi.org/10.1145/3185467.3185497

18. Peterson, R., et al.: P4Cub: a little language for big routers. In: Proceedings of the 12th ACM SIGPLAN International Conference on Certified Programs and Proofs, pp. 303–319 (2023). https://doi.org/10.1145/3554345

19. Bockenek, J.A., Verbeek, F., Lammich, P., Ravindran, B.: Formal verification of memory preservation of ×86-64 Binaries. In: Romanovsky, A., Troubitsyna, E., Bitsch, F. (eds.) SAFECOMP 2019. LNCS, vol. 11698, pp. 35–49. Springer, Cham (2019). https://doi.org/10.1007/978-3-030-26601-1_3

20. Stoenescu, R., Dumitrescu, D., Popovici, M., Negreanu, L., Raiciu, C.: Debugging P4 programs with Vera. In: Proceedings of the 2018 Conference of the ACM Special Interest Group on Data Communication, pp. 518–532 (2018). https://doi.org/10.1145/3230543.3230548

21. Strother Moore, J.: Symbolic simulation: an ACL2 approach. In: Gopalakrishnan, G., Windley, P. (eds.) FMCAD 1998. LNCS, vol. 1522, pp. 334–350. Springer, Heidelberg (1998). https://doi.org/10.1007/3-540-49519-3_22

22. The P4 Language Consortium: P4$_{16}$ language specification (2023). https://p4.org/p4-spec/docs/P4-16-v1.2.4.html

23. Tu, W., Ruffy, F., Budiu, M.: Linux network programming with P4. In: Linux Plumb. Conf (2018)

24. Tuerk, T.: A formalisation of smallfoot in HOL. In: Berghofer, S., Nipkow, T., Urban, C., Wenzel, M. (eds.) TPHOLs 2009. LNCS, vol. 5674, pp. 469–484. Springer, Heidelberg (2009). https://doi.org/10.1007/978-3-642-03359-9_32

25. Tuerk, T.: A separation logic framework for HOL. Tech. rep., University of Cambridge, Computer Laboratory (2011). https://doi.org/10.48456/tr-799

26. Wang, Q., Pan, M., Wang, S., Doenges, R., Beringer, L., Appel, A.W.: Foundational verification of stateful P4 packet processing. In: 14th International Conference on Interactive Theorem Proving (ITP 2023). Schloss-Dagstuhl-Leibniz Zentrum für Informatik (2023). https://doi.org/10.4230/LIPIcs.ITP.2023.32

Statically Inferring Usage Bounds
for Infrastructure as Code

Feitong Qiao[1]([✉]), Aryana Mohammadi[2], Jürgen Cito[3]🄳,
and Mark Santolucito[2]🄳

[1] Columbia University, New York, NY, USA
flq2101@columbia.edu
[2] Barnard College, Columbia University, New York, NY, USA
[3] TU Wien, Vienna, Austria

Abstract. Infrastructure as Code (IaC) has enabled cloud customers
to have more agility in creating and modifying complex deployments of
cloud-provisioned resources. By writing a configuration in IaC languages
such as CloudFormation, users can declaratively specify their infrastructure and CloudFormation will handle the creation of the resources. However, understanding the complexity of IaC deployments has emerged as
an unsolved issue. In particular, estimating the cost of an IaC deployment
requires estimating the future usage and pricing models of every cloud
resource in the deployment. Gaining transparency into predicted usage/-
costs is a leading challenge in cloud management. Existing work either
relies on historical usage metrics to predict cost or on coarse-grain static
analysis that ignores interactions between resources. Our key insight is
that the topology of an IaC deployment imposes constraints on the usage
of each resource, and we can formalize and automate the reasoning on
constraints by using an SMT solver. This allows customers to have formal guarantees on the bounds of their cloud usage. We propose a tool
for fine-grained static usage analysis that works by modeling the inter-
resource interactions in an IaC deployment as a set of SMT constraints,
and evaluate our tool on a benchmark of over 1000 real world IaC configurations.

Keywords: Infrastructure as Code · Static Analysis · Cost
Estimation · FinOps

1 Introduction

One of the most pressing issues with IaC deployments is in the difficulty of estimating pricing [1]. Despite cloud providers' thorough documentation of pricing
models and strong tool support, challenges remain in understanding the cost
of large deployments. In a recent industry survey, it was found that 49% of IT
executives find it difficult to get cloud costs under control, and 54% of those
believe a primary challenge is a lack of visibility into cloud usage [1]. The issue

J. Protzenko and A. Raad (Eds.): VSTTE 2024, LNCS 15525, pp. 84–95, 2025.
https://doi.org/10.1007/978-3-031-86695-1_6

of IaC analysis has also been recognized by the academic community to be of critical significance [3,5,6].

We identify two categories of existing tools for IaC cost estimation - those that rely on dynamic analysis and those that rely on static analysis. Dynamic analysis tools fall short in capturing topological changes to infrastructure, and existing static analysis tools require too much guesswork from the user.

AWS's Cost Explorer is one example of a dynamic analysis tool for IaC pricing. This tool allows users to track the ongoing usage and costs incurred of all resources in a live CloudFormation deployment. While dynamic analysis of IaC is helpful for existing infrastructure, such tools cannot be used for new deployments or topological modifications to existing infrastructure. Even a small change to the topology of an infrastructure might redirect user requests through a different path of the IaC resource graph, rendering past resource specific usage patterns irrelevant as topological changes induce a change in the dataflow.

AWS's Pricing Calculator, on the other hand, is one example of a static analysis tool for IaC pricing. This tool allows users to load a CloudFormation file, provide usage estimates, and see the anticipated cost of the overall infrastructure. However, estimating usage is extremely difficult and a regular pain point for customers. If the user is creating a new infrastructure, how can they estimate the usage? If there is a significant change to the topology of an existing infrastructure, how does the user know the extent to which past usage data can be extrapolated to the new infrastructure? Resource usage bounds can be also a useful analysis strategy for other system inquires, such as in the style of taint analysis, where a user may want to discover how one resource propagates data through the infrastructure, and which other resources are will see this data (have their usage impacted).

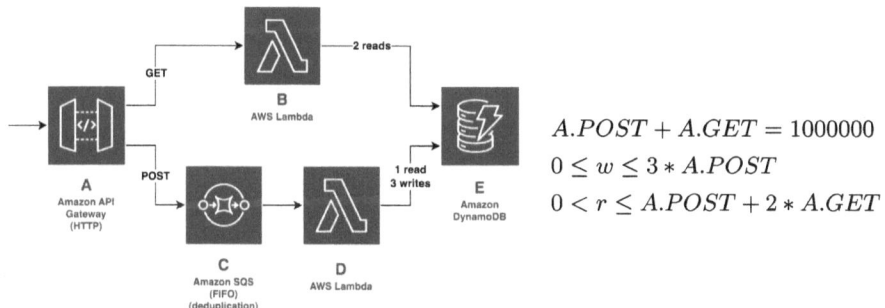

$$A.POST + A.GET = 1000000$$
$$0 \leq w \leq 3 * A.POST$$
$$0 < r \leq A.POST + 2 * A.GET$$

(a) An example CloudFormation stack topology   (b) Constraints on usage

Fig. 1. Motivating example

At a high level, we propose a static analysis method for IaC configuration files that assists users in making correct usage estimates. Our approach is, at its core, a modeling of the graph of the IaC and propagating local constraints across edges and nodes to be able to check global constraints. The key contributions of this work are:

1. a formal model of a subset of infrastructure-as-code that focuses on serverless architectures and message flow;
2. Cloudcap, a tool that models the resource usage of cloud infrastructures as a set of composable SMT constraints, allowing for user queries about validity of usage estimates and usage bounds of the overall IaC stack;
3. an evaluation on a benchmark dataset of over 1000 real world IaC files.

2   Motivating Example

As an illustrative example, consider the infrastructure depicted in Fig. 1a. Assuming that this infrastructure is new, there will be no available historical usage data. When a user wants to estimate the cost associated with this infrastructure, they must provide estimates for the utilization of each resource. Generating these estimates requires the user to manually infer the relationship between resources, such as the correlation between (A) and (E), based on the infrastructure's topology.

For instance, if we envision 1 million requests on resource (A), then the number of read requests (r) and write requests (w) on resource (E) must adhere to the system of inequalities listed in Fig. 1b. Correctly inferring these bounds requires an understanding of how every resource propagates requests through the graph, while accounting for alterations in the quantity and types of requests. Inferring this set of constraints is a non-trivial task and requires significant experience and familiarity with all the configuration options of every resource. This process only becomes more difficult with larger and more complex IaC configurations.

3   A Formal Model of IaC

Infrastructure as Code is a powerful computational model, with many different resource types for compute, storage, load balancing, etc. In order to formalize our analysis technique, we need a formal model of IaC. Since supporting the full set of resource types for any one cloud provider is an engineering effort outside the scope of this work, we present a model of a subset of an IaC system that focuses on resource usage. This is a typical strategy used in the analysis of IaC, where a formal model captures a subset of the relevant behavior and resources for the application at hand [11].

Usually, a cloud infrastructure is comprised of multiple resources (or services) that pass messages over the network to communicate with each other. Formally, an infrastructure forms a graph, where the nodes are the resources and the directed edges are the message channels from a resource to another. The resources may send messages to and receive messages from the rest of the world, thus we can regard the "world" also as a node within the graph. Upon receiving a message over an incoming edge, a node can react by sending zero or more messages over each of its outgoing edges.

To formalize this notion of IaC, let M denote the set of all messages. In a most general setting, for every node n and for each of its outgoing edges e, there exists a function $f_e : M \rightarrow \mathbb{N}$, such that upon receiving a message m, n sends $f_e(m)$ messages over e. Given a predetermined finite set of message types MT, each message m has a message type $mtype(m) \in MT$. Then for all message type t and outgoing edge e, there exists a function $g_e : MT \rightarrow \mathbb{N}$ such that for all messages m of type t, $g_e(t) = f_e(m)$. This restricts each node to always send the same number of outgoing messages for each incoming message type. In other words, the resources have a predetermined finite set of message-sending patterns that do not change over time. Note that the granularity of the model depends on what one chooses the set of message types to be.

In the current version, Cloudcap focuses on AWS serverless cloud infrastructures, supporting popular resources including (but not limited to) APIGateway, DynamoDB, SQS, SNS, S3 and Lambda. The set of message types includes a generic message type `request` that represents all messages, and also additional resource-specific message types for certain resources. For example, APIGateway has additional message types that corresponds to HTTP methods (`GET`, `POST`, `PUT`, etc.); DynamoDB has `dynamodb_read` and `dynamodb_write` message types. This set of message types is generic enough to be applied to all infrastructures using the supported resources. For future work, one can also imagine that user-defined filters in the IaC code can be utilized to populate a customized set of message types for each IaC stack.

4 System Overview

As shown in Fig. 2, our system's input is an IaC configuration provided by the user. Cloudcap uses this to build a resource graph, instantiates variables that represent the resource usage measurements, and generates constraints that relate the variables and model the message-flow behaviors within the infrastructure. It is currently implemented for the AWS CloudFormation IaC platform targeting the AWS cloud platform, but the process can be similarly applied to other IaC languages (e.g. Terraform) and cloud platforms (e.g. GCP).

4.1 Building the Resource Graph

The major cloud platforms provide a large variety of resource types. We will use RT to denote the set of resource types.

For each resource type, they receive messages of various message types. For example, an AWS DynamoDB database can receive reads and writes, and an AWS APIGateway can receive GETs and POSTs. Following Sect. 3, we denote MT to be the set of all message types (e.g. `dynamodb_read`), and use $mtypes : RT \rightarrow 2^{MT}$ to denote the assignments from a resource type to its set of message types.

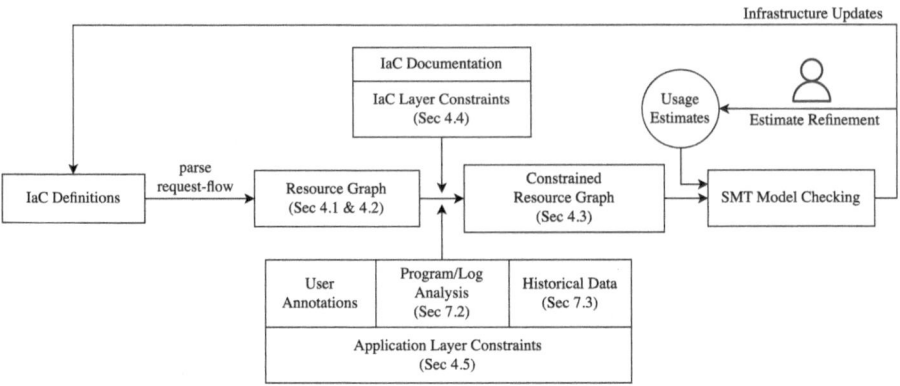

Fig. 2. System diagram

From the topology defined in the IaC definitions, we can build a resource graph, where the nodes N are the resources and the directed edges $E \subseteq N \times N$ are direct message channels. We note that the resource graph is a dataflow graph instead of a dependency graph. Unlike a IaC dependency graph in which a directed edge corresponds to a partial order of deployment [11], a directed edge in the resource graph models how a resource induces requests to specific other resources. For later use, we also define the function $rtype : N \rightarrow RT$ that retrieves each node's resource type.

4.2   Node Variables and Edge Variables

After building the resource graph from the dataflow analysis, we annotate the resource graph with variables. To model the quantitative details of the dataflow behaviors within the infrastructure, we instantiate *node variables* and *edge variables*.

A *node variable* represents the total count of a single message type received by a resource. The set of all node variables NV has a one-to-one correspondence to $\{(n, m) | n \in N, m \in mtypes(rtype(n))\}$. In other words, for each node, we instantiate a node variable for each message type associated with its resource type.

An *edge variable* represents the count of a message type that a node receives over a specific edge. The set of all edge variables EV has a one-to-one correspondence to $\{(s, t, m) | (s, t) \in E, m \in mtypes(rtype(t))\}$. In other words, for each edge, we instantiate an edge variable for each message type associated with the destination node.

To facilitate the constraint generation step next, for each node n_0, we let

- $NV(n_0) = \{v | v = (n, m) \in NV, n = n_0\}$ denote the set of node variables for n_0;
- $EV_{in}(n_0) = \{v | v = (s, t, m) \in EV, t = n_0\}$ denote the set of *incoming edge variables*, i.e. the edge variables for which n_0 is the source node;

- $EV_{out}(n_0) = \{v|v = (s, t, m) \in EV, s = n_0\}$ denote the set of *outgoing edge variables*, i.e. the edge variables for which n_0 is the destination node.

4.3 Constraint Generation

A constraint ϕ is an SMT formula such that $FV(\phi) \subseteq NV \cup EV$, where $FV(\phi)$ denotes the set of variables that occur free in ϕ. For each variable $v \in NV \cup EV$, there may be zero or more *basic* constraints that describe basic properties of the variables. At the moment, all variables have just the basic constraints that they are greater or equal to 0.

Next, for each node $n \in N$, the tool generates zero or more constraints. Each of these constraints $\phi \in C$ is categorized as one of the following:

1. **incoming**: for a node variable $nv \in NV(n)$, the constraint ϕ relates nv to the incoming edge variables, i.e. $FV(\phi) \subseteq \{nv\} \cup EV_{in}(n)$
2. **intrinsic**: the constraint ϕ relates node n's node variables to each other, i.e. $FV(\phi) \subseteq NV(n)$
3. **outgoing**: for an outgoing edge variable $ev \in EV_{out}(n)$, the constraint ϕ relates ev to its node variables, i.e. $FV(\phi) \subseteq NV(n) \cup \{ev\}$.

Intrinsic constraints capture intra-resource behavior. For example, in the motivating example Fig. 1, all incoming requests to (A) should be equal to the sum of the POST and GET requests to (A). Written as an SMT constraint, `A.requests = A.GETs + A.POSTs`.

Incoming and outgoing constraints capture inter-resource behavior. For the motivating example from Sect. 2, the number of POST requests to (A) should equal the number of requests to (C). Written as an SMT constraint, the outgoing constraint from A to C is `A.GETs = A_C.requests`. These are more difficult to derive as they can arise from both the IaC level configuration as well as the application layer (discussed in Sects. 4.4 and 4.5).

These three types of constraints allow the tool to model the system globally with only node-local knowledge. When generating constraints for a node, there is no need for graph traversal of any kind. The global set of constraints can be collected by simply iterating through the nodes.

4.4 IaC Layer Constraints

For many modern cloud serverless resources (e.g. AWS SQS and APIGateway), Cloudcap is able to generate all the necessary constraints using the information within the CloudFormation templates. Take our motivating example from Sect. 2. The node (C) is an SQS service with FIFO and deduplication enabled. By consulting the AWS documentation, we know that with these configurations, the requests that come out of (C) (and in this graph are sent to (D)) will be less than or equal to the requests sent to SQS. This induces an outgoing constraint `C.requests >= C_D.requests`. This constraint is an *IaC layer* constraint and can be derived purely from the IaC code. Every cloud resource is given a SMT constraint template, as manually derived from the documentation, that is used to generate these constraints.

4.5   Application Layer Constraints

For cloud resources with programmable behaviors, additional knowledge about the application program allows us to generate constraints that are not discoverable with just the IaC definitions. We call these *application layer* constraints. For example, in the motivating example, we have a constraint on the edge from (D) to (E) that the Lambda will induce 1 read and 3 writes to the DynamoDB (E) for every request to the Lambda. However, the information needed to generate such a constraint is beyond the scope of the IaC configuration, and thus Cloudcap is currently not able to infer application layer constraints. Cloudcap instead relies on user-provided custom SMT constraints for application layer constraints. In Sect. 7.1, we discuss some approaches one may take to automate the inference of application layer constraints.

5   Evaluation

Methodology. We draw our benchmark set from the PIPr dataset of public IaC programs [15]. PIPr contains 7104 public repositories of Programming Languages Infrastructure as Code (PL-IaC) projects written with Pulumi, AWS CDK or Terraform. With automated scripts (provided in our GitHub repository[1]), we identify the AWS CDK projects implemented in JavaScript or TypeScript, and run 'npm install; cdk synth' in each project to synthesize a CloudFormation template for each. The result is our benchmark set containing 1062 CloudFormation templates.

5.1   Quantitative Analysis

Cloudcap currently supports 12 AWS CloudFormation resource types. The tool also flags 22 resource types as non-dataflow related and omits these in the construction of the resource graph. A resource type is non-dataflow related if it is not an infrastructure resource (for instance, IAM policies and Lambda permissions). Each supported resource type typically has between 1 to 3 message types.

As a tool designed to be integrated into an existing user workflow, Cloudcap completes in a short amount of time, spending only 0.5 ± 0.15 seconds for all samples on a 32GB M1 Max MacBook Pro. As a proxy measure of complexity, we looked at the 457 templates that have at least 3 supported resource nodes, and found that the average graph degree (i.e. number of edges directed into a node) is 0.9 with a standard deviation of 0.6. This means that IaC resource graphs are usually very sparse and thus gives us confidence that Cloudcap will scale well, even with larger IaC configurations. Combined with the finding that the number of resources is usually small (benchmark set averaging 21.9 with standard deviation of 21.1), we don't expect performance to be an issue even on IaC configurations beyond our benchmark set.

---

[1] https://github.com/anonymized/anonymized.

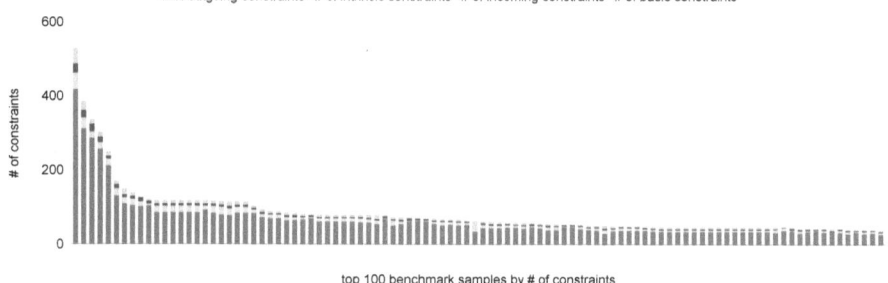

Fig. 3. Number of constraints for the benchmark samples (top 100).

We ranked the samples by the number of constraints generated by Cloudcap, and show the top 100 samples in Fig. 3. Each bar is also broken down into the four constraint types: basic, incoming, intrinsic and outgoing. This chart shows that a small number of IaC configurations have significant complexity (benchmark #1 in Fig. 3 has 529 constraints), and there is a long tail of IaC configurations that still have enough complexity such that there is value in automating this reasoning task (benchmark #100 in Fig. 3 has 39 constraints).

5.2 Sample Benchmark

To concretely demonstrate the workflow of Cloudcap, we walk through an illustrative example of a developer tasked with implementing and deploying a simple project. The project is one of our benchmarks from the PIPr dataset (ID 501027421), and is a public GitHub repository named "HektorCyC/url-shortener-app". Written in TypeScript and AWS CDK, the project is a URL shortener application, in the form of a chain from APIGateway to Lambda to DynamoDB. When run through Cloudcap, this IaC configuration has 28 constraints (ranking #138 in the benchmarks, sorted by number of constraints).

After coding up the project, the developer synthesizes a CloudFormation template named `cfn.yaml` and runs `cloudcap estimates-template cfn.yaml`. This command provides them with a template for usage estimates. After being filled in, the template looks as following:

```
apigateway :
  GETs :  100000000
  PATCHs :  100000000
  DELETEs :  100000000
dynamodb_table :
  dynamodb_reads :  3000000
```

The Lambda application receives GET, PATCH and DELETE requests from the APIGateway. For a GET request, it reads the DynamoDB once; for a PATCH or DELETE request, it reads once and writes once to the DynamoDB. The developer writes these application layer constraints as custom SMT-LIB constraints in a file named `app_constraints.smt2`, and runs `cloudcap check cfn.yaml app_constraints.smt2`. In the output, the tool reports that the user-provided estimates are invalid. The developer reviews the estimates again, discovering that they made a mistake and left out some zeros in the `dynamodb_read` usage estimate.

6   Related Work

Our work is related to cost analysis of cloud deployments and workload characterization. Workload characterization has been an active research area with a focus on understanding resource utilization, performance, and cost implications [4]. Traditional approaches to workload characterization often involve profiling applications or services to understand their resource requirements and performance characteristics. These studies typically rely on statistical analysis of historical data [2,16]. Some existing works aim at dynamic cost estimation by considering real-time resource utilization metrics and billing information. These approaches often leverage machine learning techniques to predict costs based on historical usage patterns [7,8,14]. However, they struggle to capture the intricate relationships and dependencies between resources defined in IaC deployments. Recent research has explored topology-based cost models for understanding and optimizing cloud deployments [10,12,13]. These approaches consider the arrangement and relationships between different components in an IaC deployment. However, they do not explicitly model the constraints imposed by the deployment topology and the component characteristics on resource usage. Our proposed system instead builds a topology-based resource graph to enforce constraints inherent in the component (intrinsic constraints) and the relationship between components (incoming and outgoing constraints), providing end users with formal guarantees on usage bounds.

Unlike existing approaches that predominantly rely on accurate usage estimates to provide cost estimation in cloud deployments, our system focuses on evaluating the feasibility of such estimates by modeling the intricate relationships between infrastructure components in the form of a resource graph. By employing SMT constraints to encapsulate these inter-resource interactions, our approach allows for a more rigorous examination of the deployment's constraints, informing end users whether the estimated resource usage aligns with the inherent limitations and relationships defined within the infrastructure components. This novel perspective does not only enable existing approaches to predict costs more accurately but also to ascertain the validity and appropriateness of initial usage estimates given the constraints imposed by the deployment's topology.

7   Discussion

A limitation of the evaluation is the lack of usage estimates in the benchmark. The PIPr dataset provides sufficient IaC definition samples, but does not provide corresponding resource usage estimates. Therefore, Cloudcap is not bench-marked in its capability to check them against the generated constraints. In fact, usage estimates are highly proprietary data, so they are generally not publicly available. However, we don't expect validating the usage estimates against the generated constraints to be an expensive problem.

A few software engineering issues also still need to be resolved for the tool to be adopted in industrial workflows. Often, especially in enterprise environ-ments, IaC deployments are modularized. Developing an application from mul-tiple stacks is a common and even best practice in modern IT operations [9]. However, Cloudcap requires a full view of the application's architecture to pro-vide a comprehensive set of constraints. One workaround is to create a merged template strictly for running cost estimates. Another is to constrain individual templates with Cloudcap and manually supply constraints that would connect the models together. As a novel approach to cloud resource usage analysis, a user study would help to find the to most effective ways to integrate the tool into existing usage analysis workflows.

7.1 Application Layer Constraints from Program Analysis

For resources with programmable behaviors (e.g. AWS Lambda), the IaC defini-tions are usually paired with the application source code. To extract the applica-tion layer constraints, an option is to run symbolic execution on the application source code. This might be tractable if the application is a relatively small code snippet, but will be more difficult if the program logic is complex. In the case that code analysis is not feasible, if we are updating an existing infrastructure and have log data (e.g. from the AWS Cost Explorer), we can infer some relation between the number of requests from one resource to the next. In this case, we can check the logs and see the timestamped relations between incoming requests on the neighboring nodes. The local relations on usage can be more reliably pulled from log data than global constraints, as the global relations depend on the topology of the infrastructure.

In the current version, Cloudcap focuses on the Iac layer and allows user to submit the application layer constraints as custom SMT-LIB assertions. This allows the tool to remain useful for infrastructures that utilize unsupported resources. Take the motivating example. If we replace resource (B) with an EC2 instance, Cloudcap cannot generate estimates for the entire architecture because that would require understanding the application runtime behavior. However, the user may understand that behavior and can insert correspond-ing constraints. Even in this case, the tool still greatly reduces the manual work and room for human error by taking care of the rest of the architecture.

7.2 Reusing Historical Usage Data

The static analysis and usage estimate procedure described above gives user the ability to put constraints on their infrastructure usage. However, for updates to existing infrastructure, historical usage may be available and valuable. We can incorporate this valuable data into our procedure by identifying subgraphs of the infrastructure that are minimally impacted by the IaC topological changes.

References

1. Anodot: 2022 state of cloud cost report (2022). https://go.anodot.com/2022-cloud-cost-report
2. Azmandian, F., Moffie, M., Dy, J.G., Aslam, J.A., Kaeli, D.R.: Workload characterization at the virtualization layer. In: 2011 IEEE 19th Annual International Symposium on Modelling, Analysis, and Simulation of Computer and Telecommunication Systems, pp. 63–72. IEEE (2011)
3. Böhme, L., Beckmann, T., Baltes, S., Hirschfeld, R.: A penny a function: towards cost transparent cloud programming. In: Proceedings of the 2nd ACM SIGPLAN International Workshop on Programming Abstractions and Interactive Notations, Tools, and Environments, pp. 1–10 (2023)
4. Calzarossa, M.C., Massari, L., Tessera, D.: Workload characterization: a survey revisited. ACM Comput. Surv. (CSUR) **48**(3), 1–43 (2016)
5. Cito, J., Leitner, P., Fritz, T., Gall, H.C.: The making of cloud applications: an empirical study on software development for the cloud. In: Proceedings of the 2015 10th Joint Meeting on Foundations of Software Engineering, pp. 393–403 (2015)
6. Cito, J., Piskac, R., Santolucito, M., Zaidman, A., Sokolowski, D.: Resilient software configuration and infrastructure code analysis (dagstuhl seminar 23082). Dagstuhl Reports **13**(2) (2023). https://doi.org/10.4230/DagRep.13.2.163
7. Dezhabad, N., Ganti, S., Shoja, G.: Cloud workload characterization and profiling for resource allocation. In: 2019 IEEE 8th International Conference on Cloud Networking (CloudNet), pp. 1–4. IEEE (2019)
8. Gao, J., Wang, H., Shen, H.: Machine learning based workload prediction in cloud computing. In: 2020 29th International Conference on Computer Communications and Networks (ICCCN), pp. 1–9. IEEE (2020)
9. Koskelin, J.: Modular infrastructure as code in Azure PaaS. Master's thesis, University of Helsinski (2023)
10. Leitner, P., Cito, J., Stöckli, E.: Modelling and managing deployment costs of microservice-based cloud applications. In: Proceedings of the 9th International Conference on Utility and Cloud Computing, pp. 165–174 (2016)
11. Lepiller, J., Piskac, R., Schäf, M., Santolucito, M.: Analyzing infrastructure as code to prevent intra-update sniping vulnerabilities. In: Tools and Algorithms for the Construction and Analysis of Systems: 27th International Conference, TACAS 2021, Held as Part of the European Joint Conferences on Theory and Practice of Software, ETAPS 2021, Luxembourg City, Luxembourg, March 27–April 1, 2021, Proceedings, Part II 27, pp. 105–123. Springer (2021)
12. Lin, C., Mahmoudi, N., Fan, C., Khazaei, H.: Fine-grained performance and cost modeling and optimization for FaaS applications. IEEE Trans. Parallel Distrib. Syst. **34**(1), 180–194 (2022)
13. Obetz, M., Patterson, S., Milanova, A.: Static call graph construction in {AWS} lambda serverless applications. In: 11th USENIX Workshop on Hot Topics in Cloud Computing (HotCloud 19) (2019)
14. Saxena, D., Kumar, J., Singh, A.K., Schmid, S.: Performance analysis of machine learning centered workload prediction models for cloud. IEEE Trans. Parallel Distrib. Syst. **34**(4), 1313–1330 (2023)

15. Sokolowski, D., Spielmann, D., Salvaneschi, G.: Pipr: a dataset of public infrastructure as code programs (2023). https://doi.org/10.5281/ZENODO.8262770
16. Wolski, R., Brevik, J.: Using parametric models to represent private cloud workloads. IEEE Trans. Serv. Comput. **7**(4), 714–725 (2013)

hax: Verifying Security-Critical Rust Software Using Multiple Provers

Karthikeyan Bhargavan[1]([✉]) [iD], Maxime Buyse[1], Lucas Franceschino[1],
Lasse Letager Hansen[2] [iD], Franziskus Kiefer[1], Jonas Schneider-Bensch[1],
and Bas Spitters[2] [iD]

[1] Cryspen, Paris, France
karthik@cryspen.com
[2] Aarhus University, Aarhus, Denmark

Abstract. We present hax, a verification toolchain for Rust targeted at security-critical software such as cryptographic libraries, protocol implementations, authentication and authorization mechanisms, and parsing and sanitization code. The key idea behind hax is the pragmatic observation that different verification tools are better at handling different kinds of verification goals. Consequently, hax supports multiple proof backends, including domain-specific security analysis tools like ProVerif and SSProve, as well as general proof assistants like Coq and F*. In this paper, we present the hax toolchain and show how we use it to translate Rust code to the input languages of different provers. We describe how we systematically test our translated models and our models of the Rust system libraries to gain confidence in their correctness. Finally, we briefly overview various ongoing verification projects that rely on hax.

1 Verifying Security-Critical Software

A software component is deemed security-critical if any bug or design flaw in it could be exploited by an attacker to break the security of the larger system it is a part of. This definition generally includes any code that performs operations whose inputs are partially or completely controlled by the adversary, such as code that processes packets received over an untrusted network, or code that handles an unauthenticated API call. An attacker may use the public-facing interfaces of such components to craft inputs that cause memory errors, break internal code invariants, bypass security mechanisms, and steal secrets through public interfaces or covert side-channels.

Modern software applications typically rely on a number of security-critical components, such as cryptographic libraries, protocol implementations, parsing and sanitization code, authentication and authorization mechanisms, etc. For example, every Web application relies on an implementation of the Transport Layer Security (TLS) protocol [42], which contains cryptography, protocol state machines, message parsing, and X.509 certificate-based authentication. All of this code becomes part of the trusted computing base of the application, and any bug in this code typically result in a high-profile vulnerability and expensive

© The Author(s), under exclusive license to Springer Nature Switzerland AG 2025
J. Protzenko and A. Raad (Eds.): VSTTE 2024, LNCS 15525, pp. 96–119, 2025.
https://doi.org/10.1007/978-3-031-86695-1_7

security updates. Consequently, this kind of code is usually separately audited by security experts and comprehensively tested and fuzzed before being deployed.

Formal Verification: Challenges. Given the high cost of failure, security-critical software components would, in principle, be excellent candidates for the high levels of assurance provided by formal verification and machine-checked proofs, but they come with their own unique challenges.

First of all, many security-critical components need to operate with high privileges, e.g. within operating system kernels or deep within web servers, so that they can have direct access to network buffers or to internal security mechanisms. Furthermore, they need to execute efficiently with minimal overhead, both in terms of processing time and memory usage, so that the attacker cannot overwhelm the system with junk inputs. For both these reasons, security-critical components are typically written in low-level languages like assembly or C with many platform-specific optimizations for different target architectures.

Second, these components often build upon advanced cryptographic mechanisms and protocols that require significant domain expertise to program and to analyze. Cryptographic algorithms rely on efficient implementations of mathematical structures like elliptic curves and lattices that are heavily optimized using single-instruction multiple data (SIMD) parallelization on different platforms. Protocol implementations embed complex state machines that interleave cryptographic operations with network actions and parsing code.

Consequently, to verify (say) a typical implementation of TLS, we need tools that can handle a wide range of tasks: we need to prove that its low-level assembly or C code is memory safe, that it is functionally correct with respect to some high-level mathematical specification, and that it meets its security goals against the class of attackers defined by its threat model. Although many verification tools have been developed to address subsets of these tasks, no single tool is suited to handle all of them and verifying large, complex systems remains a big challenge.

Formal Verification: Approaches. A whole field of study, sometimes called computer-aided cryptography [9], is devoted to the formal analysis of cryptographic designs and implementations, using both general-purpose software verification tools and domain-specific proof tools like symbolic protocol analyzers [11,15,18] and computational cryptographic provers [7,10,14,27].

The most successful projects in this area build customized tools for different proof tasks and link them within a single verification framework. For example, the F* verification framework [43] has been used to implement the HACL* verified cryptographic library [46], to build verified zero-copy binary parsers [41], and to perform cryptographic security proofs for a TLS implementation [20]. The code for all of these is written in a carefully designed subset of F*, verifies using custom proof libraries, and then compiled to low-level languages like C [40] and WebAssembly [39]. Similar projects link verified cryptographic assembly code written in the Jasmin language [3] with high-level security proofs in Easy-Crypt [10], or verified C code in Coq [23] with security proofs in SSProve [27], or verified JavaScript code with proofs in ProVerif and CryptoVerif [13].

Code verified using some of these projects have been widely deployed in mainstream software projects like Google Chrome, Mozilla Firefox, Linux, Python, WireGuard, etc. However, the key to their success, and also their main limitation, is that they are self contained and do not attempt to verify code written by programmers. Instead, all these projects target code written by verification researchers that are then compiled to C or assembly code that can be deployed by regular software developers who never have to see the proofs. Furthermore, the verification itself relies on deep expertise in the tools used and often takes years of effort by teams of researchers. So, while these projects show what can be done, their methods cannot scale to real-world projects driven by developers.

A key roadblock is that although several frameworks are capable of formally verifying security critical C, e.g. [5,32], and assembly, e.g. [3,16,38], however much of the time and effort for verification is usually spent in proving properties like memory safety, leaving little appetite for verifying higher-level correctness and security guarantees. Furthermore, even if one such component is fully verified, the lack of memory safety and isolation in the overall system means that any bug in another (seemingly non-security-critical) C or assembly component can break all our carefully obtained verification guarantees, by accidentally reading or overwriting the memory used by the verified code.

hax: Verifying Secure Rust Code. The advent of memory-safe systems-oriented languages like Rust has made it possible to write high-assurance high-performance code where memory safety for large swathes of code is automatically ensured by the compiler itself, allowing the programmer and reviewer to focus on higher-level properties of the code. For this reason, Rust is starting to be used in many modern security critical projects[1], operating systems[2], and web browsers[3]. Governmental organizations [1], research institutions[4], and industry bodies[5] all now heavily promote the use of memory safety languages like Rust.

There is also a vibrant community of formal verification tools for Rust code [6, 21,24,29,33,37,45]. Several of these tools explore the edges of the memory safety guarantees of Rust, such as unsafe code blocks and panic freedom. Many tools also support functional correctness reasoning via model checking or SMT solvers or general proof assistants. As yet, none of these tools support security analysis of cryptographic applications. Furthermore, all these tools are still relatively young and only time will tell which techniques will be most effective on real-world software.

In this paper, we present hax, a verification framework targeted towards the formal verification of security-critical Rust software. The development of hax began with hacspec [34], a domain-specific subset of Rust for writing and analyzing *specifications* of cryptographic algorithms. Over time, hax has evolved

---

[1] https://cryptography.rs/.

[2] https://docs.kernel.org/rust/index.html.

[3] https://security.googleblog.com/2023/01/supporting-use-of-rust-in-chromium.html.

[4] https://www.darpa.mil/program/translating-all-c-to-rust.

[5] https://www.memorysafety.org/.

to support the development, specification, and verification of *implementations* of more general security mechanisms written in idiomatic Rust.

The key features that drive the design of hax are:

- **Support for multiple provers**, including general-purpose proof assistants and security-oriented analyzers for cryptographic code;
- **Formal specifications** for correctness and security embedded within the source Rust code and translated to each proof backend;
- **Formal Rust library model** written and specified once in Rust and translated to each proof backend;
- **Programmer-driven verification** that allows the Rust programmer to embed lemmas, annotations, and proofs within the Rust code and keep them consistent as the code evolves;
- **Translation validation via testing** which allows the programmer and verification engineer to execute and test both the Rust code and the generated models in various backends to gain assurance in the correctness of the hax engine and library models.

In particular, hax does not promote a single verification framework and instead makes it easy to add new proof backends for different target domains. At the same time, hax takes charge of the technical tasks of processing and simplifying the input Rust code, modeling the Rust standard libraries, and providing an integrated development and verification environment for Rust developers that scales.

2   hax: Methodology and Workflow

Figure 1 depicts the high-level architecture of the hax framework. The programmer provides a Rust crate containing some code and a formal specification for the code written as pre- or post-conditions, invariants, assertions, or lemmas within the source code. The user would typically also provide tests that can be run on the code. When this crate is compiled, the Rust compiler translates the Rust code to assembly, links it with the Rust standard library and any other external crates the user may rely on, and produces an executable that runs the tests.

The first phase of the hax toolchain is the hax frontend, which plugs into the Rust compiler and uses it to parse and typecheck the source Rust code before producing a fully annotated abstract syntax tree (AST) for the crate as a JSON file. The frontend is capable of producing both the Typed High-Level Intermediate Representation (THIR) and the Mid-Level Intermediate Representation (MIR) of Rust. Since the Rust compiler and its internal data structures evolve fairly rapidly, the frontend takes on the responsibility of keeping track of compiler changes while producing a stable AST that other tools can use. As a result, the hax frontend is an independently useful tool and is also used by other Rust verification frameworks like Aeneas [28].

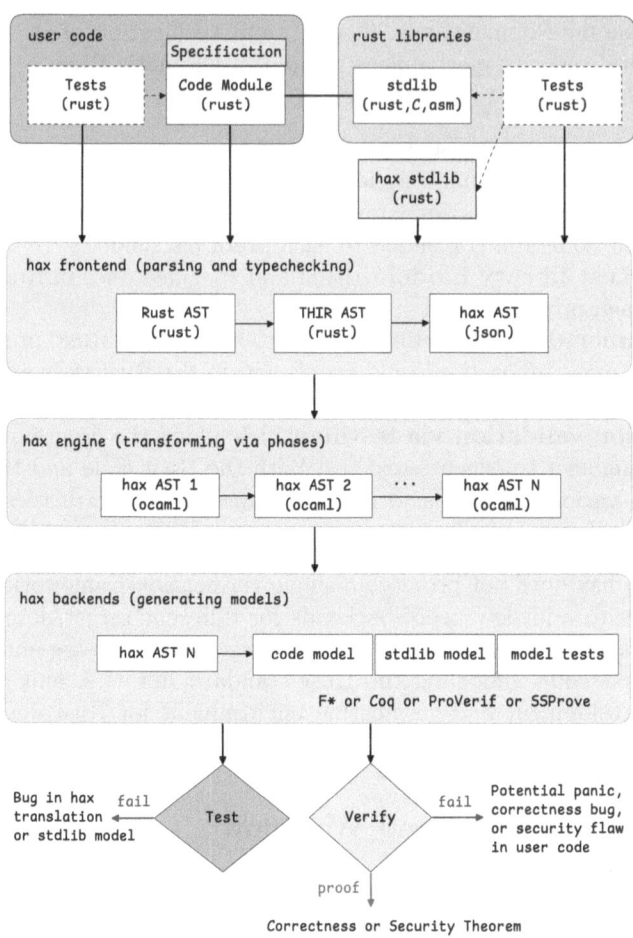

Fig. 1. hax architecture

The second phase is the hax engine, which imports the Rust THIR AST for a crate and transforms it via a sequence of *phases* to a simplified AST that can be directly translated to the input languages of various backends. We will describe some of these phases in Sect. 3.

In the final phase, hax passes on the simplified program to the backend chosen by the programmer. For example, if the programmer chooses F*, the F* backend of hax will generate a purely functional model of the source Rust code and its specification in F*. This model is then linked with F* models of the Rust standard library (and any other external crates) and can be verified for panic freedom and functional correctness against the high-level specification. Completing the proof may require additional annotations, such as loop invariants, or calls to mathematical lemmas. A verification failure may indicate an incomplete proof or a bug in the source code. Other proof backends, such as ProVerif, are completely automated and will either verify the code to produce a security theorem, or generate a counter-example. We describe our current backends in Sect. 4.

We use hax to translate not just the user code, but also handwritten abstract models of the Rust standard library from Rust to various backends. This allows us to model the library once and automatically obtain consistent models for each backend. Modeling the Rust standard library is an incremental, continuous community-driven process. We currently support a few commonly-used libraries, and allow the programmer to extend the library either in Rust or directly in their chosen backend. More details on our model of the Rust libraries are given in Sect. 5.

Our goal is for all these translations in the hax engine and backends to be well-documented and auditable, but we notably do not yet provide formal guarantees for their correctness, which would require us to formalize the semantics of the source Rust and each target language in a proof framework. Instead, we aim to provide pragmatic guarantees based on testing. The generated code for some backends (such as F* and Coq [44]) is executable, so we can compile the tests from the source code to the proof backend and run them to check that the input-output behavior is the same. This gives us additional confidence in the translation and in our model of the Rust standard library. We describe this testing strategy in Sect. 6.

Several projects are using hax to formally verify real-world software. We briefly mention some of these projects in Sect. 7.

The hax project is developed as a community-driven open source project and all our code, libraries, and examples are available online at:

https://github.com/hacspec/hax

3 hax Engine: Transforming and Simplifying Rust Code

The hax engine takes as its input the AST produced by the frontend, which is close to the Rust THIR AST, except that all types, trait information, and attributes are inlined. It then performs a series of passes on this AST, called *phases*, that transform the Rust code to a simplified form that is suitable for translation to a proof backend.

3.1 Input Rust AST

Fig. 2e presents the input AST in extended Backus-Naur form (EBNF). This figure captures the syntax of Rust as received by the hax engine from the frontend. It includes all the familiar constructions from Rust, but does not include features like macros that are eliminated by the Rust compiler.

Literals (`literal`) include strings, integers, booleans, and floating point numbers (although most of our backends do not have any support for floats).

Types (`ty`) include the Rust builtin types: characters, strings, booleans, integers (of size 8, 16, 32, 64, 128 bits or pointer-sized), and floats (16, 32, or 64 bit). They also include composite types such as tuples, fixed length arrays, variable

```
string ::= char*
digit ::= [0-9]
uint ::= digit+
int ::= ("-")? uint
float ::= int (".")? uint
bool ::= "true" | "false"


local_var ::= ident
global_var ::= rust-path-identifier

literal ::=
| "\"" string "\""
| "'" char "'"
| int
| float [d]
| bool

generic_value ::=
| "'" ident
| ty
| expr


goal ::=
|

ty ::=
| "bool"
| "char"
| "u8" | "u16" | "u32" | "u64"
| "u128" | "usize"
| "i8" | "i16" | "i32" | "i64"
| "i128" | "isize"
| "f16" | "f32" | "f64" [d]
| "str"
| (ty ",")*
| "[" ty ";" int "]"
| "[" ty "]"
| "*const" ty | "*mut" ty [a]
| "*" expr | "*mut" expr [a]
| ident
| (ty "->")* ty
| dyn (goal)+ [d]

pat ::=
| "_"
| ident "{" (ident ":" pat ";")* "}"
| ident "(" (pat ",")* ")"
| (pat "|")* pat
| "[" (pat ",")* "]" [b]
| "&" pat
| literal
| ("&")? ("mut")? ident ("@" pat)? [c]

modifiers ::=
| ""
| "unsafe" modifiers
| "const" modifiers
| "async" modifiers [a]

guard ::=
| "if" "let" pat (":" ty)? "=" expr
```

```
expr ::=
| "if" expr "{" expr "}" ("else" "{" expr "}")?
| "if" "let" pat (":" ty)? "=" expr "{" expr "}" (
  "else" "{" expr "}")?
| expr "(" (expr ",")* ")"
| literal
| "[" (expr ",")* "]" | "[" expr ";" int "]"
| ident "{" (ident ":"expr ";")* "}"
| ident "{" (ident ":"expr ";")* ".." expr "}"
| "match" expr guard "{"
  (("|" pat)* "=>" (expr "," | "{" expr "}"))*
  "}"
| "let" pat (":" ty)? "=" expr ";" expr
| "let" pat (":" ty)? "=" expr "else" "{" expr "}"
  ";" expr
| modifiers "{" expr "}"
| local_var
| global_var
| expr "as" ty
| "loop" "{" expr "}" [e]
| "while" "(" expr ")" "{" expr "}" [e]
| "for" "(" (pat "in" expr ")" "{" expr "}" [e]
| "for" "(" "let" ident "in" expr ".." expr ")" "{
  " expr "}" [e]
| "break" expr
| "continue"
| pat "=" expr
| "return" expr
| expr "?"
| "&" ("mut")? expr [c]
| "&" expr "as" "&const _" [a]
| "&mut" expr "as" "&mut _"
| "|" pat "|" expr

impl_item ::=
| "type" ident "=" ty ";"
| modifiers "fn" ident ("<" (generics ",")* ">")?
  "(" (pat ":" ty ",")* ")" (":" ty)? "{" expr "}"

trait_item ::=
| "type" ident ";"
| modifiers "fn" ident ("<" (generics ",")* ">")?
  "(" (pat ":" ty ",")* ")" (":" ty)? ("{" expr "}"
  | ";")

item ::=
| "const" ident "=" expr
| "static" ident "=" expr [a]
| modifiers "fn" ident ("<" (generics ",")* ">")?
  "(" (pat ":" ty ",")* ")" (":" ty)? "{" expr "}"
| "type" ident "=" ty
| "enum" ident ("<" (generics ",")* ">")? "{" (
  ident ("(" (ty)* ")")? "," )* "}"
| "struct" ident ("<" (generics ",")* ">")? "{" (
  ident ":" ty ",")* "}"
| "trait" ident ("<" (generics ",")* ">")? "{" (
  trait_item)* "}"
| "impl" ("<" (generics ",")* ">")? ident "for" ty
  "{" (impl_item)* "}"
| "mod" ident "{" (item)* "}"
| "use" path ";"
```

Fig. 2. hax Input Rust AST in EBNF. (a) no support yet for raw pointers, async/await, static, extern, or union types.(b) partial support for nested matching and range patterns.(c) partial support for mutable borrows.(d) most backends lack support for dynamic dispatch, floating point operations.(e) some backends only handle specific forms of iterators.

length slices, function types, and named types defined by enums and structs. We currently do not support raw pointer types or dynamic dispatch.

Patterns (`pat`) allow matching over the supported types: wildcards, literals, arrays, records, tuples etc. with some limitations in the support for nested patterns and range patterns.

Expressions (`expr`) include literals, variables, type conversions, assignments, array and type constructor applications, and control flow expressions such as conditionals, pattern matches, loops, blocks, and closures. They also include referencing, dereferencing, mutably borrows, and raw pointer operations, although the engine currently does not support raw pointers and only offers limited support for mutable borrows. Specifically, we do not currently support user-written functions that return mutable borrows. Although the engine can handle any kind of loop expression, many of our backends (e.g. ProVerif) have very limited support for loops and so the backend code may impose restrictions on the forms of loops it will accept.

Items (`item`) are the top-level construct in a module and include constants, function definitions, type definitions, trait definitions, trait implementations, modules, and imports. We do not support global static pointers, and we do not model the asynchronicity of `async` functions.

A Rust crate consists of a set of (potentially mutually-recursive) modules, each of which consists of a list of items. A crate may refer to external crates and to the Rust standard library. The engine treats each crate independently: to analyze the crate, we assume that all its dependencies have either been translated or have been modeled by hand for the target backend.

3.2   Transformation Phases

A phase is a typed transformation of AST items: each phase takes a typed AST representing a Rust crate and produces a new typed AST after rewriting some items. The full list of phases implemented by the engine is documented in the source code[6]. Here, we focus on the most important transformations implemented by sets of phases:

- **Order and Bundle Items and Modules.** Rust offers programmers a high degree of flexibility in referencing code and items within and across modules. For example, an item can refer to another item that appears later in the module, or an item within any other module or crate. One can define mutually recursive functions within modules and across modules, but even without recursion, there may be cyclic dependencies between modules. Conversely, most backend proof languages (including all the ones we currently support) allow these kinds of dependencies. Consequently, the engine implements phases that reorder and bundle mutually recursive items so that every item's dependencies occur before it in the AST. For modules with cyclic dependencies, the engine breaks the cycle by creating a big bundled module with the contents of all the modules in the cycle.

---

[6] https://hacspec.org/hax/engine/hax-engine/Hax_engine/Phases/index.html.

– **Eliminate Local Mutation.** Rust functions can declare local mutable variables and modify them in conditional and loop expressions, but this kind of mutation is not supported by some backends. The engine contains a phase that eliminates local mutation and replaces it by shadowing. That is, the mutation of a variable x gets replaced with a `let` expression that defines a new instance of x with the updated value. This transformation is propagated through blocks, loops, and function bodies, so that each expression returns a pair consisting of its original return value and the set of updated values for all mutable variables it modifies. This state-passing transformation is quite straightforward and was also used e.g. in hacspec [34] and Aeneas [29].

– **Eliminate Mutable Borrows.** Each Rust function can have mutably borrowed inputs, mutably borrowed outputs, and local mutable borrows within the function body. The engine implements a transformation that rewrites functions that use mutable borrows as arguments into a state-passing style (in a similar spirit to the elimination local mutation). Conversely, hax has only limited support for functions that create or return mutable borrows. In general, such borrows are only supported as long as they do not create aliases; that is, as long as the mutable borrows are immediately used as function arguments, in which case they are rewritten in a state-passing style.

– **Simplify Control Flow.** Rust programs may contain any combination of conditional, match, and loop expressions, where any deeply nested expression could contain a `return`, `break`, or `continue` which can cause the control flow to jump several layers outwards. Rust also supports the question mark (?) operator that automatically propagates errors out from deep within a function. Most backend provers do not have such expressive control flow, and consequently, the engine implements a set of phases that rearranges expressions so that all these kinds of return expressions are always in leaf position in the control flow graph and so the control flow of each expression is simplified and made explicit in the syntax.

– **Functionalize Iterators.** The Rust compiler desugars all the loop constructions in its surface syntax, such as `for` and `while` loops, into a generic `loop` construction over a generic iterator. The engine implements a phase that propagates the state-passing transformation to loops so that they get transformed into a state-passing `fold` construction that modifies an accumulator at each iteration of the loop. Since proofs about loops often require the most manual intervention, the engine also implements phases that identify common loop patterns and translates them to specialized `fold` constructions. For example, a `for` loop over a range is translated in a way that it is trivial to show that it terminates.

3.3 Choosing and Composing Phases

The hax engine is designed to be modular in that it can be used to execute different sequences of phases to obtain different results. Each phase has a set of preconditions, expressed in terms of features it expects to be present or absent in the input AST, and a post-condition that describes how it changes these features.

These constraints are enforced in the engine using typed OCaml functors and feature variables that together ensure that only sensible compositions of phase transformations can be created.

For each backend, we choose a specific set of phases. For example, to translate Rust code to purely functional models in F* and Coq, we use all the phases described above. ProVerif supports more flexible control flow, so we do not need to perform the control flow transformation. SSProve supports local mutation, and so we do not transform local mutation, while we still use the other phases. Finally, each backend may only have limited support for certain features, like loops or floating point numbers. In these cases, the engine leaves it to the backend to identify and reject code that uses unsupported features.

4 hax Backends: Translating Rust to Verifiable Models

Once the hax engine has transformed the input Rust code into a suitable form, we can use the corresponding backend implementation to emit a model in the input language for some prover. The hax backend framework provides a set of convenient libraries that make it easy to add new backends. This includes utilities for formatting the output, mapping locations between the output model and the input Rust source code, and other visualisation and dependency analysis tools that can be shared between backends.

To add a backend, we need to implement rules for translating various syntactic elements (items, expressions, types, etc.) into the corresponding syntax of the target prover. We illustrate how this works for four backends: F*, Coq, SSProve, and ProVerif. Backends for others provers such as EasyCrypt and Lean are currently under development.

4.1 F*

F* [43] is a proof-oriented programming language that has been used to develop verified software for a variety of projects, including cryptography [46], protocols [20], and parsing [41]. Code written in F* can be compiled to OCaml for testing and execution, and some subsets of F* can be compiled to C [40] and WebAssembly [39]. To develop a proof in F*, the user annotates the F* program with assertions, refinement types, invariants, pre- and post-conditions, and lemmas. These are then formally proved using F*'s dependent type system, with the assistance of the Z3 SMT solver [35].

We illustrate the F* backend of hax with an example. Below is a function that implements the Barrett reduction for signed 32-bit integers. This function is taken from a new Rust implementation of the ML-KEM post-quantum cryptographic standard [2] that uses hax for formal verification.

```
1   #[hax::requires((i64::from(value) >= -BARRETT_R && i64::from(value) <= BARRETT_R))]
2   #[hax::ensures(|result| result > -FIELD_MODULUS && result < FIELD_MODULUS &&
3                       result % FIELD_MODULUS == value % FIELD_MODULUS)]
4   pub fn barrett_reduce(value: i32) -> i32 {
5       let mut t = i64::from(value) * BARRETT_MULTIPLIER;
6       t += BARRETT_R >> 1;
7       let quotient = t >> BARRETT_SHIFT;
8       let sub = (quotient as i32) * FIELD_MODULUS;
9       hax::fstar!(r"Math.Lemmas.cancel_mul_mod (v $quotient) 3329");
10      value - sub
11  }
```

Barrett reduction is a commonly-used algorithm in implementations of modular arithmetic. Here, the function takes an input of type i32 and performs a series of arithmetic and bitwise operations on it (multiplications, shift-right, addition, subtraction) that implement a modular reduction with respect to the constant FIELD_MODULUS (which here is the prime 3329). The reader might wonder why do not directly use the remainder operator of Rust (%). The reason is that division and remainder are not constant-time operations—their execution time may depend on the value of their inputs—and hence are vulnerable to side-channel attacks that may the potentially secret input value. Indeed, such attacks have been found on similar function in ML-KEM implementations [12].

Panic Freedom. It is also important to remember that while Rust programs are memory safe, they can still panic. In the code above, unless we can prove that every multiplication, addition, and subtraction produces results that are within the target type, the code will potentially panic on some inputs and never return a result. For example, for any input greater or equal to 2147468668 the barrett reduction function above goes out of bounds on line 8 and Rust panics (in debug mode). So, when defining a hax backend, we need to decide whether to generate the model in a way that the programmer must *intrinsically* prove that the code never panics, or to produce a model that may panic and allow the programmer to reason about panics *extrinsically* via lemmas. Different backends may make different choice. In the F* backend we always prove panic-freedom and so ask the programmer to add pre-conditions on the input to ensure the absence of panics.

Correctness Specification. We add a specification to the function in the form of a pre-condition and post-condition. The pre-condition (hax::requires) says that the input is within a given range (here -2^{26} <= value <= 2^{26}). The post-condition (hax::ensures) says that the output computes the signed modulus of the input with respect to the FIELD_MODULUS. Proving that the function meets this specification requires a prover that can reason about the mathematical and bitwise operations in the code as well as modular arithmetic.

F* Translation. When we use hax to translate the Rust code above to F*, we obtain the model in Fig. 3. There are several notable elements in this translation:

– The Rust compiler elaborates all the type conversions and arithmetic operations to the corresponding library calls, such as core::convert::from and core::ops::arith::neg::neg and adds the relevant type annotations. These

```
 1  let barrett_reduce (value: i32)
 2      : Prims.Pure i32
 3      (requires
 4        (Core.Convert.f_from #i64 #i32 #FStar.Tactics.Typeclasses.solve value <: i64) ≥
 5        (Core.Ops.Arith.Neg.neg v_BARRETT_R <: i64) &&
 6        (Core.Convert.f_from #i64 #i32 #FStar.Tactics.Typeclasses.solve value <: i64) ≤
 7        v_BARRETT_R)
 8      (ensures
 9        λresult →
10          let result:i32 = result in
11          result ≥ (Core.Ops.Arith.Neg.neg v_FIELD_MODULUS <: i32) &&
12          result ≤ v_FIELD_MODULUS &&
13          (result %! v_FIELD_MODULUS <: i32) = (value %! v_FIELD_MODULUS <: i32)) =
14    let t:i64 =
15      (Core.Convert.f_from #i64 #i32 #FStar.Tactics.Typeclasses.solve value <: i64) *!
16      v_BARRETT_MULTIPLIER
17    in
18    let t:i64 = t +! (v_BARRETT_R ≫! 1l <: i64) in
19    let quotient:i64 = t ≫! v_BARRETT_SHIFT in
20    let sub:i32 = (cast (quotient <: i64) <: i32) *! v_FIELD_MODULUS in
21    let _:Prims.unit = Math.Lemmas.cancel_mul_mod (v quotient) 3329 in
22    value −! sub
```

Fig. 3. Barrett Reduction function translated to F* by hax

are then translated by the F* backend to the corresponding library functions modeled in F* (e.g. Core.Convert.f_from).

– The pre-condition and post-condition get translated to the corresponding **requires** and **ensures** clauses in F*.

– All mathematical operations are translated to the *strict* versions of these operations in F* (e.g. +! ,−! ,*! ,≫!) which have pre-conditions stating that their inputs must be within certain ranges to prevent panics.

– Local mutability for the variable t (line 6 in Rust) gets translated to variable shadowing in F* (line 18 in Fig. 3).

F* Proof. The F* typechecker is able to automatically prove that the code does not panic by using the Z3 SMT solver to reason about the arithmetic operations and their bounds. In fact, it can prove that the function will not panic for any input from -2147468667 to 2147468667. To prove the post-condition, however, we need to use a mathematical property about modular multiplication called cancel_mul_mod in the F* libraries. We inject a call to this lemma within the source Rust code at line 9 and it gets translated to the F* model. With this lemma call, the F* typechecker is able to verify the function.

Backend Features. We have illustrated the F* translation by one example, but more generally, the generated programs in the Pure (i.e. total, terminating, side-effect-free) fragment of the F* language. Since F* is usually more expressive than Rust, most of the translations are straightforward: enums translate to algebraic data types, structs to records, traits to typeclasses, etc. The F* backend includes models for many commonly-used Rust features and libraries, but does not support reasoning about raw pointers or mutable borrows that have not been eliminated by the engine.

4.2 Coq

Coq, recently renamed Rocq, is a fully-featured interactive theorem prover with a rich history and a large user community. Notably, Coq has a small kernel for checking proofs and hence has a much smaller trusted base compared to F* which relies on the correctness of both its typechecker and the Z3 SMT solver.

The Coq backend is very similar to the F* backend, with superficial differences in the notations and libraries used in Coq. By translating Rust code to Coq, we can prove the same kinds of properties as in F* (panic-freedom, functional correctness) but using the tactic-based interactive proof style of Coq. Some examples on the use of the hax Coq backend are given in [26].

4.3 SSProve

The SSProve tool [27] supports computational security proofs about cryptographic constructions, using a technique called State Separating Proofs (SSP) [17]. SSProve is structured as a library within Coq that defines an embedded imperative domain specific language (DSL) that allows mutable local variables, random sampling, and various cryptographic and mathematical operations.

The backend for SSProve follows the same structure as for Coq, except that it produces code within the SSProve DSL, which is restricted to a smaller set of types. Notably SSProve does not support enums and structs, so we need to encode these using tuples and sum types.

Security Proofs with SSProve. To show the use of the SSProve backend, we will go through a simple example also used in the last yard [26]. The example is the classic one-time pad (OTP) construction, implemented in Rust using the XOR operation:

```
1   fn xor(a : u64, b : u64) -> u64 {
2     let x : u64 = a;
3     let y : u64 = b;
4     x ^ y
5   }
```

The SSProve backend translates this Rust function into the following definition in SSProve (within Coq):

```
1   Definition xor (a : both int64) (b : both int64) : both int64 :=
2     xor a b :=
3       letb (x : int64) := a in
4       letb (y : int64) := b in
5       x .^ y : both int64.
```

Next, we model the ideal behavior of this function. That is a purely mathematical formulation of the desired behavior. The idealized function is written by hand in SSProve as follows

```
Definition ideal_xor (a : both int64) (b : both int64) : both int64 :=
  ret_both (is_pure a ⊕ is_pure b)
```

To follow the methodology for state-separating proofs (SSP) [17], we modularize each function into a *package* to isolate its behavior. A *game*, a pair of packages indexed by a Boolean value, is defined from the real and ideal packages

```
Definition IND_CPA_game :=
  fun b ⇒ if b then ideal_xor_package else xor_package.
```

Our security statement is: given the above game, it is impossible to find the value of the Boolean, regardless of how you interact with the resulting package. The best you can do is guess. This is called IND-CPA security. In SSProve, this security statement is written as follows:

```
Theorem uncondition_security : ∀ A, Advantage IND_CPA_game A = 0.
```

Linking SSProve with Coq. When proving, it is often useful to have a translation between the imperative SSProve code and the functional Coq code, so that, for example, we can compute functions without needing to interpret the SSProve code, or we can use existing Coq libraries. The SSProve backend automatically generates translations between the generated SSProve and Coq models, along with proofs of equality between the two, allowing the programmer to freely switch between the two backends and safely compose their proofs.

4.4 ProVerif

ProVerif [15] is an automated security protocol verification tool, where protocols are modeled in the applied π-calculus. Given such a protocol model and security goals (such as confidentiality, authentication, privacy) stated as *queries* over the model, ProVerif uses sophisticated algorithms to automatically verify that the protocol satisies these goals against a large class of *symbolic* or Dolev-Yao adversaries [22]. This threat model is one where the adversary can perform unbounded computatation, start and control any number of protocol sessions, read any message sent over the public network, and construct and send messages of any size.

In terms of cryptography, the symbolic model of ProVerif is less precise than the probabilistic computational model used in SSProve: it cannot guess secrets and must treat all cryptographic operations as perfect black boxes. Conversely, this abstraction allows ProVerif to automatically verify a large class of protocols which would require painstaking manual proofs in computational proof backends.

Implementing Protocols. As an example, consider the following Rust function taken from a protocol implementation. Here, the initiator function takes some input keying material (`ikm`) and a pre-shared key (`psk`); it derives an encryption key and initialization vector (`response_key_iv`); it serializes and encrypts this value with the pre-shared key; and it returns the key and a message (`initiator_message`) that must be sent over the public network to the peer.

```
1  pub fn initiate(ikm: &[u8], psk: &KeyIv) -> Result<(Message, KeyIv), Error> {
2      let response_key_iv = derive_key_iv(ikm, RESPONSE_KEY_CONTEXT)?;
3      let serialized_responder_key = serialize_key_iv(&response_key_iv);
4      let initiator_message = encrypt(psk, &serialized_responder_key)?;
5      Ok((initiator_message, response_key_iv))
6  }
```

A protocol implementation typically consists of a list of such functions, each of which either processes or produces a protocol message, using some internal state, cryptographic operations (like `encrypt`) and parsing/serialization functions.

```
1    letfun proverif_psk__initiate(ikm : bitstring, psk : proverif_psk__t_KeyIv) =
2         let response_key_iv = proverif_psk__derive_key_iv(
3            ikm, proverif_psk__v_RESPONSE_KEY_CONTEXT
4         ) in (
5            let serialized_responder_key =
6              proverif_psk__serialize_key_iv(response_key_iv)
7            in
8            let initiator_message = proverif_psk__encrypt(
9              psk, serialized_responder_key
10           ) in (initiator_message, response_key_iv)
11           else bitstring_err()
12        )
13        else bitstring_err().
```

Fig. 4. ProVerif Translation of Protocol Initiator

The security goals of the protocol implementation are typically expressed in terms of confidentiality—which variables must remain secret from the adversary–and authentication—which variables must be protected from tampering by unauthorized parties. In the function above, we may wish to ask that `response_key_iv` must remain secret as long as the `psk` is secret, even if the attacker get to read (and tamper) with the `initiator_message` (or any other message sent over the public network).

ProVerif Translation. The Rust function above is translated to a function macro on ProVerif, as depicted in Fig. 4. Here, calls to the `derive_key_iv` and `encrypt` functions are translated to calls to our cryptographic library model in ProVerif, where they are modeled using symbolic constructors and destructors.

Serialization and parsing functions, like `serialize_key_iv`, can either be modeled using tuples, constructors, and pattern matching, or the user can abstract them as opaque constructors, depending on the precision of analysis desired.

The translation also shows how certain control-flow constructions in Rust are transformed by the engine and the backend. On lines 2 and 4 of the Rust code, we see the question-mark operator of Rust. This means that the expressions on these lines can return an error and if they do, then the function immediately returns with an error result. These lines are transformed by the hax engine so that they have a more explicit control flow, which is then reflected in the generated ProVerif model, which returns explicit errors when functions fail.

Automated Protocol Security Analysis. To verify security properties on the ProVerif model, we extend the generated model with a verification scenario and security goals as shown below:

```
1    free PSK: proverif_psk__t_KeyIv [private].
2    free SECRET_PAYLOAD: bitstring [private].
3    query attacker(PSK).
4    query attacker(SECRET_PAYLOAD).
5    process
6       Initiator(PSK) | Responder(PSK, SECRET_PAYLOAD)
```

Here, `Initiator` and `Responder` are ProVerif processes that call the functions extracted from the Rust code for the two parties in the protocol. Both share a global secret variable `PSK` containing the pre-shared key, and the responder also has a secret payload it encrypts back to the initiator.

The two confidentiality queries ask whether an attacker would be able to obtain the pre-shared key or the secret payload. ProVerif is able to automatically analyze the model and prove that these values are indeed secret. We can also further extend the model and study the security of the protocol with an arbitrary number of keys and payloads, where some pre-shared keys may be compromised, etc. and ProVerif will be able to either prove security or provide a counter-example with a symbolic attack. In some cases, especially where the protocol contains some logical loops or recursive data structures, ProVerif may not terminate and the user would need to encode some abstractions for analysis to terminate.

ProVerif is just one of the many protocol verificaiton tools available in the literature. In the future, one could consider targeting other such verifiers by adding backends for them, or for languages like SAPIC+ language [18] that unify many such tools under a common syntax.

5 Formal Models for Rust Libraries

Rust programs rely on a number of builtin features and libraries provided by the Rust compiler and the standard libraries: `core`, `alloc`, and `std`.

Primitive types, like machine integers, and operators on them are defined within the compiler. The core library defines a minimal set of features needed by most Rust programs. The alloc library builds on top of core and handles memory allocation and some basic data structures. The std library uses core and alloc to provide a number of data structures.

These libraries are large: core is ~60,000 lines of Rust code (~2300 public functions); alloc is another ~27,500 lines (~800 public functions); and std is ~92,000 lines (~3900 public functions). Not all these libraries are written in Rust; some of them use wrappers around external C and assembly libraries.

To formally verify a Rust program, we must therefore provide models for all its dependencies, including the Rust standard libraries and external third-party crates. Of course, it would be even more desirable to formally verify these external dependencies (see e.g. one ongoing effort to verify std[7]), but even modeling the public functions in these libraries is a mammoth task that requires an incremental community effort.

In the context of `hax`, we need to provide models of the libraries for each backend, which can be both a tedious task and risks creating inconsistencies between different backends. To this end, we employ two strategies towards modeling the Rust libraries. For a minimal set of primitive types and functions, we manually write models for each backend in a way that maximally leverages existing libraries and abstractions in that backend. For higher-level libraries, we write

---

[7] https://github.com/model-checking/verify-rust-std.

models in Rust and compile them using hax itself to generate consistent libraries for each backend.

Hand-written Models for Primitive Types. Many types and functions that are primitive to Rust still need to be mapped to the corresponding types and constructions in various backends. This includes:

- machine integers (e.g. u8, i16, etc.), booleans, strings
- slices and arrays ([T], [T; N]})
- options, results, and panic
- iterators (loop, map, enumerate, etc.)

For each backend we need to manually write the translation of these primitives; see Fig. 5 for how some of them are mapped in the Coq backend.

```
fn primitives() {                                Definition primitives '(_ : unit) : unit :=
  // bool                                           let _ : bool := (false : bool) in
  let _: bool = false;                              let _ : bool := (true : bool) in
  let _: bool = true;

  // Numerics                                        let _ : t_u8 := (12 : t_u8) in
  let _: u8 = 12u8;                                  let _ : t_u16 := (123 : t_u16) in
  let _: u16 = 123u16;                               let _ : t_u32 := (1234 : t_u32) in
  let _: u32 = 1234u32;                              let _ : t_u64 := (12345 : t_u64) in
  let _: u64 = 12345u64;                             let _ : t_u128 := (123456 : t_u128) in
  let _: u128 = 123456u128;                          let _ : t_usize := (32 : t_usize) in
  let _: usize = 32usize;                            let _ : t_i8 := (-12 : t_i8) in
                                         ⟹          let _ : t_i16 := (123 : t_i16) in
  let _: i8 = -12i8;                                 let _ : t_i32 := (-1234 : t_i32) in
  let _: i16 = 123i16;                               let _ : t_i64 := (12345 : t_i64) in
  let _: i32 = -1234i32;                             let _ : t_i128 := (123456 : t_i128) in
  let _: i64 = 12345i64;                             let _ : t_isize := (-32 : t_isize) in
  let _: i128 = 123456i128;
  let _: isize = -32isize;                           let _ : float := (1.2%float : float) in
                                                     let _ : float := ((-1.23)%float : float) in
  let _: f32 = 1.2f32;
  let _: f64 = -1.23f64;                             let _ : ascii := ("c"%char : ascii) in
                                                     let _ : string := ("hello world"%string : string) in
  // Textual                                         tt.
  let _: char = 'c';
  let _: &str = "hello world";
}
```

Fig. 5. Primitives translated to Coq

A key requirement for these hand-written models is that they must be executable, so that we can run and test both these libraries and the code that uses them. Of course, we also need these models to be suitable for verification, and so we often extend these libraries with all the necessary lemmas and tactics to help the user prove properties about their programs.

Generating Library Models from Rust. For most libraries in core, alloc, and std, we advocate writing models of the library directly in Rust and compiling these models to each backend.

In effect, we build a new version of these libraries, layered on top of the Rust standard libraries, but shadowing the namespaces so that we can link them to unmodified Rust code. For example, we implement the `Add` trait in `core::ops`, as a new `hax-core::ops::Add`, and translate it via hax to obtain models of `core::ops` in each backend.

To implement traits like `Add` generically for all machine integers in Rust, we first build an architecture for the mathematical interpretation of rust types. We define a Rust library for mathematical integers (represented by the type `HaxInt`), and for each machine integer of type `T`, we define a method `lift()` that computes its underlying integer (`HaxInt`) and a method `lower()` that casts a mathematical integer into the machine integer (if it is within bounds, and panics otherwise).

This notion of abstracting (or lifting) and concretizing (or lowering) Rust data types into mathematical structures is generally useful for writing formal models in Rust and we systematically use it in our library models.

We can now specify libraries like `core::num` and `core::ops` directly in Rust, by lifting the inputs to mathematical integers, doing the operations on `HaxInt` and lowering the result back to machine integers. For example, the equality operation on u8 is defined in Rust as an implementation of the `PartialEq` trait. We model it in Rust as follows (using a type wrapper `U8`):

```
1  impl<'a> PartialEq for U8<'a> {
2    fn eq(&self, rhs: &Self) -> bool {
3      compare_fun(self.clone().lift(), rhs.clone().lift())
4        == Ordering::Equal
5    }
6  }
```

This then gets translated to each backend using the definitions of `lift`, `lower`, and mathematical integers in that backend. For example, the Coq translation is as follows. The trait implementation translates to a typeclass instance that operates on Coq integers.

```
1  Instance t_PartialEq_774173636 : t_PartialEq (( t_U8)) (( t_U8)) :=
2  {
3    PartialEq_f_eq := fun  (self : t_U8) (rhs : t_U8) ⇒
4      PartialEq_f_eq
5        (haxint_cmp
6          (Abstraction_f_lift (Clone_f_clone (self)))
7          (Abstraction_f_lift (Clone_f_clone (rhs))))
8        (Ordering_Equal);
9  }.
```

The F* implementation is similar, while in ProVerif, all machine integers are modeled as mathematical integers, so lifting and lowering are identity functions.

Mixing the Two Styles. For each library, we always have the choice between using the automatically generated model or manually writing models for different backends. Where possible, we prefer generated libraries, since they require less work and keep libraries consistent between different backends. However, in some cases we may want to exploit some data structure or proof library that is available in a specific backend. In such cases, we often start with the generated library and then edit it to exploit features of the backend. For example, in the Coq translation above we could replace `haxint_cmp` with the comparison operation in Coq, which might result in simpler proofs.

6   Testing the Generated Models

The hax toolchain implements a sequence of translations from Rust to various formal languages. There are many ways of gaining confidence that the models generated by hax correctly capture the semantics of the input Rust code.

One could formalize the semantics of the source and target languages and prove that the translation preserves the observable behaviors of the program. This kind of proof effort can be valuable but requires significant effort and is less feasible for frameworks like hax that support multiple, widely different backends.

Instead, we take a more pragmatic approach of using a mixture of testing and proof to get more assurance in our methodology.

Verifying Library Annotations. For each function in the Rust library, our library models provide pre- and post-conditions that specify whether and when these functions may panic and what they compute. For the core library functions, we also add specification of various useful properties, and prove these properties for out library models. When generating library models, we can add these lemmas in the Rust source so that they are reflected in all backends.

A simple example is commutativity of addition:

```
#[hax_lib::lemma]
fn add_comm(x: u8, y: u8) -> Proof<{ x + y == y + x }> {}
```

This generates a lemma that must be proven for each backend library.

We have added such lemmas for associativity, commutativity, distributivity, negation, etc. for various combinations of arithmetic and bitwise operators for various numerical types. We define similar lemmas about concatenation and slicing of arrays and slices. These lemmas gives us more confidence that the annotations we use for our proofs are sound with respect to our library models.

Testing Source Annotations. In addition to proving lemmas about source code (and library) annotations, we can also use these annotations to drive property-based tests. We systematically use the `QuickCheck` [19] framework to automatically generate tests based on the pre- and post-conditions on the Rust source code. In particular, this technique is used to generate hundreds of tests for each function in our Rust standard library model, including our models for each arithmetic operation.

Testing Generated Models. An important feature of the many hax backends is that the generated models are executable, and hence testable. So, when we compile some Rust code to (say) F*, we also compile its tests and run them on the generated F*. This gives us confidence in the hax translation and in our (executable) library models.

For example, [26] presents a reference implementation of the AES cryptographic algorithm in Rust, and shows how it can be compiled via the hax toolchain to SSProve. We test this AES implementation in both Rust and in Coq/SSProve to prove that the encryption and decryption produce the same result in the source code and target model.

Linking Different Models. Another way of gaining confidence in our translations is to formally link the models produced via independent translations. For example, our SSProve backend actually consists of two translations. A functional translation, which is very close to the Coq backend (but uses a smaller universe of types); and an imperative translation with state, making use of the domain specific language (DSL) for code in SSProve. The translations are combined into language constructions, with a projection to each of the translations and a proof of equality between them [26]. In a sense the main difference between the two translation is that one of them uses a few extra functionalization phases, so this proof can be seen as a proof of correctness for those phases.

7   Verifying Rust Applications with hax

The hax verification framework is used by several projects for the specification and verification of security and correctness properties. In this section, we give a brief overview of some of these applications.

hacspec. hacspec[8] is a purely functional subset of Rust that can be used, together with a specification library, to write succinct, executable, and verifiable specifications in Rust, that can then be translated into various formal languages using hax. It has been proposed as a general specification language for IETF and NIST standards [8].

The hacspec language has recently also been adopted by Crux-Mir [37], a cross-language verification tool for Rust and C/LLVM. Crux-MIR has been used to verify the Ring library implementations of SHA-1 and SHA-2 against their hacspec specifications.

Libcrux. The libcrux library [31] provides a uniform API for formally verified cryptographic implementations in Rust, C, and assembly. It uses hacspec to specify the correctness of its implementations and presents a safe, defensive Rust API to applications. Recently, the post-quantum key encapsulation mechanism ML-KEM [36] was added to libcrux[9]. It was verified using hax and its F* backend. This implementation has since been adopted by OpenSSH and by Mozilla for use in its NSS cryptographic library.

---

[8] https://hacspec.org.
[9] https://cryspen.com/post/ml-kem-implementation/.

In [30], hax' Coq backend is used to connect the Fiat-cryptography [23] verified compiler for finite field arithmetic in Coq. In this way, a simple specification/reference implementation in hacspec can be compiled to a highly optimized implementation in many C-like languages, such as C, Rust, Java, etc. This code has also been integrated into libcrux.

Bertie. hax is used to extract a ProVerif model from the TLS 1.3 implementation in Bertie[10] to perform a symbolic security analysis[11]. hax is also used to compile the parsing and serialization code of Bertie to F* in order to prove panic freedom and functional correctness.

Smart contracts. Rust is a popular smart contract language, as it allows one to efficiently compile to Wasm which is a popular on-chain virtual machine. In [25], hax has been used to verify properties of Rust smart contracts using the ConCert smart contract verification framework [4] in Coq. This is combined with cryptographic proofs in SSProve.

8   Conclusion and Future Work

We have presented hax: a developer-oriented framework for verifying security critical Rust code. Verification can be done in a wide spectrum of proof backends, ranging from tools for generic program verification (F* and Coq) to symbolic protocol analyzers (ProVerif) and provers for computational cryptography (SSProve). We use a combination of testing and proving to gain assurance that our specifications, translations, and library models are correct. The hax toolchain is being used in many active projects, both in industry and academia.

The design is hax makes it compatible and extensible with other proof methodologies and backend provers. The hacspec language is used in Crux-Mir, the hax frontend is used in Aeneas, and the specifications used in hax are compatible with Kani and Creusot. Moreover, our backend framework makes it easy to add new backends. In future work, we would like to add new backends for Easy-Crypt and Lean, as well as explore fully automated tools for verifying generic Rust code.

References

1. Back to the building blocks: a path towards secure and measurable software (2024). https://www.whitehouse.gov/wp-content/uploads/2024/02/Final-ONCD-Technical-Report.pdf
2. Module-Lattice-based key-encapsulation mechanism standard (2024). https://doi.org/10.6028/NIST.FIPS.203
3. Almeida, J.B., et al.: Jasmin: high-assurance and high-speed cryptography. In: CCS, pp. 1807–1823. ACM (2017)

---

[10] https://github.com/cryspen/bertie.
[11] https://cryspen.com/post/hax-pv/.

4. Annenkov, D., Nielsen, J.B., Spitters, B.: Concert: a smart contract certification framework in COQ. In: CPP, pp. 215–228. ACM (2020)
5. Appel, A.W.: Verified software toolchain. In: Goodloe, A., Person, S. (eds.) NASA Formal Methods - 4th International Symposium, NFM 2012, Norfolk, VA, USA, April 3-5, 2012. Proceedings. LNCS, vol. 7226, p. 2. Springer (2012). https://doi.org/10.1007/978-3-642-28891-3_2
6. Astrauskas, V., Müller, P., Poli, F., Summers, A.J.: Leveraging rust types for modular specification and verification. In: Object-Oriented Programming Systems, Languages, and Applications (OOPSLA), vol. 3, pp. 147:1–147:30 (2019)
7. Baelde, D., Delaune, S., Jacomme, C., Koutsos, A., Lallemand, J.: The squirrel prover and its logic. ACM SIGLOG News **11**(2), 62–83 (2024)
8. Barbosa, M., Bhargavan, K., Kiefer, F., Schwabe, P., Strub, P., Westerbaan, B.: Formal specifications for certifiable cryptography (2024)
9. Barbosa, M., et al.: Sok: computer-aided cryptography. In: SP, pp. 777–795. IEEE (2021)
10. Barthe, G., Dupressoir, F., Grégoire, B., Kunz, C., Schmidt, B., Strub, P.: Easycrypt: a tutorial. In: FOSAD. LNCS, vol. 8604, pp. 146–166. Springer (2013)
11. Basin, D.A., Cremers, C., Dreier, J., Sasse, R.: Tamarin: verification of large-scale, real-world, cryptographic protocols. IEEE Secur. Priv. **20**(3), 24–32 (2022)
12. Bernstein, D.J., et al.: KyberSlash: exploiting secret-dependent division timings in Kyber implementations. Cryptology ePrint Archive, Paper 2024/1049 (2024). https://eprint.iacr.org/2024/1049
13. Bhargavan, K., Blanchet, B., Kobeissi, N.: Verified models and reference implementations for the TLS 1.3 standard candidate. In: 2017 IEEE Symposium on Security and Privacy, SP 2017, San Jose, CA, USA, May 22-26, 2017, pp. 483–502. IEEE Computer Society (2017). https://doi.org/10.1109/SP.2017.26
14. Blanchet, B.: Cryptoverif: computationally sound mechanized prover for cryptographic protocols. In: Dagstuhl Seminar Formal Protocol Verification Applied, vol. 117, p. 156 (2007)
15. Blanchet, B.: Automatic verification of security protocols in the symbolic model: the verifier proverif. In: FOSAD. LNCS, vol. 8604, pp. 54–87. Springer (2013)
16. Bond, B., et al.: Vale: verifying high-performance cryptographic assembly code. In: Kirda, E., Ristenpart, T. (eds.) 26th USENIX Security Symposium, USENIX Security 2017, Vancouver, BC, Canada, August 16-18, 2017, pp. 917–934. USENIX Association (2017). https://www.usenix.org/conference/usenixsecurity17/technical-sessions/presentation/bond
17. Brzuska, C., Delignat-Lavaud, A., Fournet, C., Kohbrok, K., Kohlweiss, M.: State separation for code-based game-playing proofs. In: Peyrin, T., Galbraith, S. (eds.) ASIACRYPT 2018. LNCS, vol. 11274, pp. 222–249. Springer, Cham (2018). https://doi.org/10.1007/978-3-030-03332-3_9
18. Cheval, V., Jacomme, C., Kremer, S., Künnemann, R.: SAPIC+: protocol verifiers of the world, unite! In: USENIX Security Symposium, pp. 3935–3952. USENIX Association (2022)
19. Claessen, K., Hughes, J.: Quickcheck: a lightweight tool for random testing of Haskell programs. In: ICFP, pp. 268–279. ACM (2000)
20. Delignat-Lavaud, A., et al.: Implementing and proving the TLS 1.3 record layer. In: 2017 IEEE Symposium on Security and Privacy, SP 2017, San Jose, CA, USA, May 22-26, 2017, pp. 463–482. IEEE Computer Society (2017). https://doi.org/10.1109/SP.2017.58

21. Denis, X., Jourdan, J.H., Marché, C.: Creusot: a foundry for the deductive verification of rust programs. In: International Conference on Formal Engineering Methods, pp. 90–105. Springer (2022)
22. Dolev, D., Yao, A.C.: On the security of public key protocols. IEEE Trans. Inf. Theory **29**(2), 198–207 (1983)
23. Erbsen, A., Philipoom, J., Gross, J., Sloan, R., Chlipala, A.: Simple high-level code for cryptographic arithmetic - with proofs, without compromises. In: IEEE Symposium on Security and Privacy, pp. 1202–1219. IEEE (2019)
24. Gäher, L., Sammler, M., Jung, R., Krebbers, R., Dreyer, D.: Refinedrust: a type system for high-assurance verification of rust programs. Proc. ACM Program. Lang. **8**(PLDI), 1115–1139 (2024)
25. Hansen, L.L., Spitters, B.: Specifying smart contract with Hax and concert. In: CoqPL (2024). https://popl24.sigplan.org/details/CoqPL-2024-papers/9/Specifying-Smart-Contract-with-Hax-and-ConCert
26. Haselwarter, P.G., Hvass, B.S., Hansen, L.L., Winterhalter, T., Hritcu, C., Spitters, B.: The last yard: foundational end-to-end verification of high-speed cryptography. In: CPP, pp. 30–44. ACM (2024)
27. Haselwarter, P.G., et al.: SSProve: a foundational framework for modular cryptographic proofs in COQ. ACM Trans. Program. Lang. Syst. **45**(3), 15:1–15:61 (2023)
28. Ho, S., Boisseau, G., Franceschino, L., Prak, Y., Fromherz, A., Protzenko, J.: Charon: an analysis framework for rust. arXiv preprint arXiv:2410.18042 (2024)
29. Ho, S., Protzenko, J.: Aeneas: rust verification by functional translation. PACM PL **6**(ICFP) (2022). https://doi.org/10.1145/3547647
30. Holdsbjerg-Larsen, R., Spitters, B., Milo, M.: A verified pipeline from a specification language to optimized, safe rust. In: CoqPL'22 (2022). https://popl22.sigplan.org/details/CoqPL-2022-papers/5/A-Verified-Pipeline-from-a-Specification-Language-to-Optimized-Safe-Rust
31. Kiefer, F., et al.: HACSPEC: a gateway to high-assurance cryptography. Real-WorldCrypto (2023)
32. Kroening, D., Schrammel, P., Tautschnig, M.: CBMC: the C bounded model checker. arXiv preprint arXiv:2302.02384 (2023)
33. Lehmann, N., Geller, A.T., Vazou, N., Jhala, R.: Flux: liquid types for rust. Proc. ACM Program. Lang. **7**(PLDI), 1533–1557 (2023)
34. Merigoux, D., Kiefer, F., Bhargavan, K.: Hacspec: succinct, executable, verifiable specifications for high-assurance cryptography embedded in Rust, Technical report, Inria (2021). https://inria.hal.science/hal-03176482
35. de Moura, L.M., Bjørner, N.S.: Z3: an efficient SMT solver. In: Ramakrishnan, C.R., Rehof, J. (eds.) Tools and Algorithms for the Construction and Analysis of Systems, 14th International Conference, TACAS 2008, Held as Part of the Joint European Conferences on Theory and Practice of Software, ETAPS 2008, Budapest, Hungary, March 29-April 6, 2008. Proceedings. LNCS, vol. 4963, pp. 337–340. Springer (2008)
36. NIST: Module-lattice-based key-encapsulation mechanism standard, Technical report, Federal Information Processing Standards Publications (FIPS PUBS) 203, U.S. Department of Commerce, Washington, D.C. (2024). https://doi.org/10.6028/NIST.FIPS.203
37. Pernsteiner, S., et al.: Crux, a precise verifier for rust and other languages. arXiv preprint arXiv:2410.18280 (2024)

38. Polyakov, A., Tsai, M., Wang, B., Yang, B.: Verifying arithmetic assembly programs in cryptographic primitives (invited talk). In: Schewe, S., Zhang, L. (eds.) 29th International Conference on Concurrency Theory, CONCUR 2018, September 4-7, 2018, Beijing, China. LIPIcs, vol. 118, pp. 4:1–4:16 (2018)

39. Protzenko, J., Beurdouche, B., Merigoux, D., Bhargavan, K.: Formally verified cryptographic web applications in webassembly. In: 2019 IEEE Symposium on Security and Privacy, SP 2019, San Francisco, CA, USA, May 19-23, 2019, pp. 1256–1274. IEEE (2019). https://doi.org/10.1109/SP.2019.00064

40. Protzenko, J., et al.: Verified low-level programming embedded in F. Proc. ACM Program. Lang. **1**(ICFP), 17:1–17:29 (2017). https://doi.org/10.1145/3110261

41. Ramananandro, T., et al.: Everparse: verified secure zero-copy parsers for authenticated message formats. In: 28th USENIX Security Symposium, USENIX Security 2019, Santa Clara, CA, USA, August 14-16, 2019, pp. 1465–1482. USENIX Association (2019)

42. Rescorla, E.: The Transport Layer Security (TLS) Protocol Version 1.3. RFC 8446 (2018). https://doi.org/10.17487/RFC8446

43. Swamy, N., et al.: Dependent types and multi-monadic effects in F*. In: Bodík, R., Majumdar, R. (eds.) Proceedings of the 43rd Annual ACM SIGPLAN-SIGACT Symposium on Principles of Programming Languages, POPL 2016, St. Petersburg, FL, USA, January 20 - 22, 2016, pp. 256–270. ACM (2016). https://doi.org/10.1145/2837614.2837655

44. The Coq Development Team: The Coq proof assistant (2024). https://doi.org/10.5281/zenodo.11551307

45. VanHattum, A., Schwartz-Narbonne, D., Chong, N., Sampson, A.: Verifying dynamic trait objects in rust. In: Proceedings of the 44th International Conference on Software Engineering: Software Engineering in Practice, pp. 321–330 (2022)

46. Zinzindohoué, J.K., Bhargavan, K., Protzenko, J., Beurdouche, B.: Hacl*: a verified modern cryptographic library. In: Thuraisingham, B., Evans, D., Malkin, T., Xu, D. (eds.) Proceedings of the 2017 ACM SIGSAC Conference on Computer and Communications Security, CCS 2017, Dallas, TX, USA, October 30 - November 03, 2017, pp. 1789–1806. ACM (2017). https://doi.org/10.1145/3133956.3134043

Author Index

J. Protzenko and A. Raad (Eds.): VSTTE 2024, LNCS 15525, p. 121, 2025.
https://doi.org/10.1007/978-3-031-86695-1